OFFICE-HOLDERS IN MODERN BRITAIN

X
Officials of Royal Commissions
of Inquiry 1870-1939

OFFICE-HOLDERS
IN MODERN BRITAIN

Volumes I-VI compiled by J.C. Sainty;
Volumes VII-VIII compiled by J.M. Collinge

I
Treasury Officials
1660-1870 (1972)

II
Officials of the Secretaries
of State
1660-1782 (1973)

III
Officials of the Boards
of Trade
1660-1782 (1974)

IV
Admiralty Officials
1660-1870 (1975)

V
Home Office Officials
1782-1870 (1975)

VI
Colonial Office Officials
1794-1870 (1976)

VII
Navy Board Officials
1660-1832 (1978)

VIII
Foreign Office Officials
1782-1870 (1979)

IX
Officials of Royal
Commissions of Inquiry
1815-1870 (1984)

The above volumes, the first five of which were formerly published by the Athlone Press, are now published and distributed by the University of London, Institute of Historical Research, Senate House, London WC1E 7HU

OFFICE-HOLDERS
IN MODERN BRITAIN

X

# Officials of Royal Commissions of Inquiry 1870-1939

compiled by
Elaine Harrison

UNIVERSITY OF LONDON
INSTITUTE OF HISTORICAL RESEARCH
1995

*Published by*
UNIVERSITY OF LONDON
INSTITUTE OF HISTORICAL RESEARCH
*Senate House, London WC1E 7HU*


© University of London 1995


**British Library Cataloguing-in-
Publication Data.
A catalogue record for this book is
available from the British Library.**


ISBN 1 871348 29 3

*Printed in Great Britain by*
Quorn Selective Repro Limited, Loughborough, LE11 1HH

# Acknowledgements

I am indebted to a great many people for help in the compilation of this book: the archivists and staff of the Public Record Office, House of Lords Record Office, British Library (in particular Mr Richard Cheffins who drew my attention to the 1887 RC on Malta), Oriental and India Office Library, University of London Library, British Library of Political and Economic Science, and a number of Government Departments. Mr Lloyd of the Records Division of the Home Office elucidated various procedural matters; Ms Karen George of MAFF, Mr Ian Hill of the Scottish Record Office, and especially Mr Richard Ponman of the Historical and Records Section of the Cabinet Office gave me much useful information. Ms Mithu Alur helped me to index the names of Indian Commissioners. I am grateful to Mrs Joyce Horn, Professor Jane Lewis, and Sir John Sainty for their advice and encouragement. Any errors of fact or interpretation are mine.

# Contents

# Abbreviations

| | |
|---|---|
| ADM | Admiralty |
| App. | Appointed |
| Asst. | Assistant |
| Bd. | Board |
| BT | Board of Trade |
| C., Cd., Cmd. | Command Paper |
| CAB | Cabinet |
| Comm. | Commission |
| cr. | created |
| d. | died |
| Dept. | Department |
| Est. | Estimated |
| HO | Home Office |
| ktd. | knighted |
| LGB | Local Government Board |
| LP | Letters Patent |
| LPGS | Letters Patent under the Great Seal |
| m. | married |
| MAF | Ministry of Agriculture and Fisheries |
| Min. | Ministry |
| P.P. | Parliamentary Paper(s) |
| pres. | presented (to Parliament) |
| PRO | Public Record Office |
| Pt. | Part |
| RC | Royal Commission |
| Rep. | Reported |
| repr. | representing; represented |
| RSM&S | Royal Sign Manual & Signet |
| Rs. | Rupees |
| Sec. | Secretary |
| subsq. | subsequently |
| succ. | succeeded |
| T | Treasury |
| vol. | volume |
| Warr. | Warrant |

# Note on Editorial Method

This volume lists British Royal Commissions appointed between 1870 and the Second World War. It differs from its predecessor[1] in that it is not confined to Royal Commissions into subjects concerning England and Wales. It lists Scottish Commissions, and those Irish, Indian and Colonial inquiries which were appointed as Royal rather than Vice-Regal Commissions. It also gives brief details of permanent, semi-permanent and electoral commissions.[2]

The arrangement of this book uses the same broad format as the previous volume: the introduction is followed by entries detailing individual Royal Commissions, with separate indexes for names of Commission personnel, and Commissions.

The main part of the book consists of entries on each British Royal Commission which was appointed between 1870 and the Second World War, and gives the date of appointment; the number of the report where appropriate; the date when the report was signed, or the date of its presentation to Parliament if no date for signature was given; the sessional year if relevant; the Command number of the report; volume and page number. Where a Command number is followed by a hyphen and one or more small roman numerals or there are two successive Command numbers before a volume number, this indicates that the report is followed by Minutes of Evidence, appendices, etc. If there are several volumes of evidence and ancillary documents these have been referenced separately from the reports under the general heading of 'other papers', and give the sessional year, Command number and volume number (page numbers have not been included): see, for example, the 1894 Commission on Labour. After 1921 evidence was published separately as non-Parliamentary papers, and for a number of years the references give the year of publication and the heading used in the Consolidated Index to non-Parliamentary papers. From the the mid-1930s the more usual practice was to index the evidence for Royal Commissions under the name of the Commission itself. This inconsistent method of referencing has been adopted partly for reasons of space, but also because of the lack of a standard format in the reporting of Commissions. Costs are taken from the Parliamentary Returns and from the estimates which were required to be printed with the reports after 1921.

---

[1] *Officials of Royal Commissions of Inquiry 1815-70*, comp. J.M. Collinge (1984).

[2] See Appendix 1.

During this period most Royal Commissions were issued under the Royal Sign Manual, and only variations from this practice have been noted. These were usually Colonial Commissions which were written under the Royal Sign Manual and Signet, and some Scottish Commissions issued under Letters Patent under the Great Seal and counter-sealed in Edinburgh.

The titles and surnames of Commissioners are given in the order in which they appear on the Warrants of appointment, with the chairman being named first; full forenames and the family names of Bishops and Peers are given in the name index. Dates of death are given only when the person died during the course of the Commission. The names of the Secretary and Assistant Secretaries, together with their usual profession or Government department where known, follow the names of Commissioners; if a Secretary was named in the Warrant this is indicated. Changes in membership and terms of reference are listed, together with the dates of the Warrants which recorded them. The dates of knighthoods or elevations to the peerage are recorded within the entries if they occurred during the person's service on a Commission, and in the index if they were between Commissions. The names of Assistant Commissioners have been noted when included in the reports, and where it was possible to trace full names for the majority of them.

The specific terms of reference have been abbreviated when they are more than a few sentences in the original Warrant, and except in very extensive cases follow the same format and wording. The first words are printed in bold to distinguish the terms of reference from any subsequent text, and the spelling of inquire/enquire is that used on the Warrants. In general only the names of those who signed minority reports or reservations to majority reports are given; it should be assumed that all other Commissioners signed the majority report.

Appendix 1 lists a number of Royal Commissions which do not fit into the general classification scheme used in this book, and is in four sections. The first lists Commissions established to arrange or co-ordinate Britain's contribution to international exhibitions; these were generally presided over by the current Prince of Wales and often included other members of the royal family, offering a rather less contentious form for royal involvement than social inquiries.[3] They often had many members, and only their president and/or chairman, and secretary are listed here. The second category are those Commissions of a permanent or semi-permanent nature which are listed with their first chairman, first report, and last report if closed before 1940. The third section follows the same format as the main part of the book and gives details of the two Special Commissions into the conduct of the War in Dardanelles and Mesopotamia. The final section is a list of the Commissions set up to inquire into electoral corruption, giving only the

[3]See no. **82**.

date, place and number of the report.

The first three sections are indexed in the name index with an 'A' preceding their number in the appendix. The election Commissions have not been indexed.

# Introduction

This book lists the personnel of most British Royal Commissions of Inquiry appointed between 1870 and 1940. For reasons of space it omits the members of the various Commissions appointed in connection with International Exhibitions, and into allegations of electoral corruption. Brief details of these are given in the appendices, and their members can be traced through the Parliamentary reports listed there. The starting date for the book is the point at which the previous listing in this series[1] stopped and the final date is the outbreak of the Second World War. The dating for other books in the series relates to the civil service reforms of the 1860s and 1870s, but these did not greatly affect the appointment of Royal Commissioners.[2] This introduction offers a brief summary of the procedures for appointing Commissions and the organisation of their work during the period, and largely uses material from the Home Office and Treasury files on specific Commissions held at the Public Record Office. It should be emphasised that this survey is extremely cursory; the relevant files are often incomplete and not fully indexed; and much material on Royal Commissions may be found within Departmental files which have not been consulted for the purposes of this book. Furthermore, since Secretaries and Chairmen frequently retained Commission papers at their discretion these may be held within various archives.

Royal Commissions occupy a distinctive position in the administration of the British state. Their members are not office-holders in the same sense as those who are listed in other volumes in this series, although individually they may have held civil service or government positions. Very few Royal Commissions had any enforceable legal powers; they could not compel witnesses either to appear before them, or to produce documents; they could recommend legislative action, but had no authority to implement it.[3] Yet they continued to

---

[1]*Officials of Royal Commissions of Inquiry 1815-70*, comp. J.M. Collinge (1984).

[2]Although there were some implications for the appointment of administrative staff as will be shown here.

[3]During the 1870-1940 period six RCs were appointed to carry out the provisions of specific Acts of Parliament (nos. **31, 49, 100, 123, 172** and **195**). Nos. **67** and **128** were supported by Acts of Parliament which gave them additional powers to compel attendance of witnesses; these powers were also given to no. **185** under the provisions of the 1921 Tribunals of Inquiry Act. Four RCs were given administrative or executive powers under war-time regulations (nos. **161, 162, 163** and **167**). The RC into the Transvaal (no. **42**) apparently had considerable executive powers which do not seem to have been granted

occupy considerable amounts of executive and administrative time, and public money until well into the 20th century when they were largely replaced by other forms of *ad hoc* inquiry such as Departmental[4] and inter-departmental committees. There were also very many of them: over 130 Royal Commissions were appointed between 1870 and 1900; sixty-one between 1900 and 1914; and fifty-nine from 1914 to 1940, with an average membership of seven and a minimum administrative staff of three. The other forms of government inquiry were equally numerous; for example, there were about seventy Departmental Committees between 1877 and 1900.[5] Such inquiries were temporary, and although they operated within parameters set by the government, they were not departments of state.[6] In this sense each one was unique, and any history of them must necessarily be episodic rather than narrative, particularly since the contents of the surviving records are so inconsistent.[7]

Royal Commissioners held their appointment directly from the Crown, even though their members were invariably government nominees. The relative number of Commissions appointed during the period does not seem to have

---

by a specific statute.

[4]The use of Departmental Committees is difficult to trace since their reports were customarily regarded as confidential documents, although since the late 19th century they have usually been presented to Parliament. (See Todd, *On Parliamentary Government*, 1877, Vol.1, p. 452.) The first Departmental Committee listed in the Ford *Breviates* (see n. 5 below) is the 1877 inquiry into the Legal Business of Government; they seem to have been used infrequently during the next decade but increased rapidly in the 1890s when they outnumbered Royal Commissions.

[5]The numbers of Departmental Committees are taken from the *Breviates of Parliamentary Papers, 1900-16; 1917-39; 1940-54*, ed. P. & G. Ford (Oxford, 1957, 1951 and 1961 respectively), and are approximate since the Fords were primarily concerned to give details of those inquiries which dealt with social and economic matters.

[6]The status of Royal Commissions was addressed by a Treasury Memorandum by R. Ferguson of 13 Oct. 1877: 'Temporary Commissions, are they Departments of State'. This was written mainly as an attempt to clarify whether or not the staffs of RCs were required to possess or obtain Civil Service certificates of competence. Ferguson stated that this was 'not a matter of law *but only of Treasury practice*. This question was fully discussed in 1870 and we then held that a Temporary C. is not a Dept. of the Civil Service within the meaning of clause II of the Order in Council of the 4th June 1870.' (PRO.T.1.7646A (16154))

[7]The most complete record of the activities of individual Royal Commissions is the Treasury index T.108; even though many of the files listed there have not survived, the ledger entries give descriptions of their contents.

varied greatly under successive governments although overall there was a continued decline; for example, the Conservative administration of 1874-80 appointed twenty-seven while the slightly shorter Liberal government of 1880-85 appointed eighteen. Incoming governments did not normally suspend arrangements previously in place for the appointment of Commissions: for example the Royal Commissions on the Blind; Poor Laws; and Food Prices were issued within days of a new administration. Commissions were initiated by Government Departments, most usually the Home Office whose General Department[8] was always responsible for drawing up the Warrants of appointment.[9] These gave the full names, titles, and status of each Commissioner; the terms of reference; and the formal parameters of the inquiry. They were usually signed by the Home Secretary and by the Colonial or War Secretary in the case of inquiries relating to those Departments,[10] but were never issued until formal approval had been obtained from the monarch.[11] They were thus authoritative and imposing State documents, theoretically forming individual and direct contracts of temporary employment between monarch and subject, with the government, in the person of the appropriate Secretary of State, merely acting as intermediary. Any subsequent changes of either the personnel or the terms of reference occasioned a new Warrant, which was usually issued in a shortened

---

[8]This subsequently became and remains the responsibility of the Constitutional Department of the Home Office.

[9]The Treasury file on the RC on Lunacy of 1924 (T.160/196) has one of the fullest records of the background to the appointment of a Royal Commission.

[10]There were a number of anomalies: the RC into Opium (no. **85**) was signed by the Colonial Secretary; the first Warrants for the RC into Indian Expenditure (no. **91**) were signed by the Secretary of State for India, while later Warrants for this Commission and all subsequent Indian Commissions were signed by the Home Secretary. The RC into Martial Law in South Africa (no. **112**) was signed by the Colonial Secretary; but the RC into Military Preparation for the South African War (no. **113**) was signed by the Home Secretary, as were a number of other RCs concerned with military matters at this time (nos. **116** and **117**). The practice for Scottish Commissions seems to be related to the instruments by which they were appointed: if RSM they were signed by the Home Secretary and after 1885 the Scottish Secretary; if LPGS they were signed jointly by the Deputy Keeper of the Seal and the Director of Chancery.

[11]The Departmental Committee into the Procedure of Royal Commissions (1910, Cd. 5235, lviii, 371) set out a number of procedural recommendations which were incorporated into successive Home Office guidelines; these, together with a Home Office notice to RC Secretaries of 1968, remain in use today. (HO letter to author of 4 Apr 1995) PRO.HLG. 10/2 contains a memo of 22 July 1927 from D. Veale (Private Secretary to the Minister of Health) to I.F. Armer (Secretary to the RC on London Squares) elaborating on the instructions for procedure.

form, although there seems to have been no consistent practice here.[12] When there were frequent changes of personnel, as in the Royal Commission on Natural Resources (no. **151**), the successive shorter Warrants were consolidated into a more comprehensive document which reprinted the names of all serving Commissioners and the terms of the original Commission.

From 1870 all Commissions into English, Welsh and Irish affairs were issued by a Warrant under the Royal Sign Manual;[13] this was also the case for Indian Royal Commissions (nos. **85, 91, 137, 153, 156, 183, 187, 190, 195** and **198**). The Colonial Commissions[14] appointed during this period were written under the Royal Sign Manual and Signet, apart from the Royal Commission on Malta (no. **203**) and the Royal Commission into Australian Meat Exports (no. **159**).[15] Scottish Commissions alone were inconsistent: some were issued under Royal Sign Manual, but others were issued under Letters Patent and countersealed in Edinburgh.[16] Before 1870 Dr Collinge has noted that there

---

[12]See no. **91**.

[13]Todd notes that the practice of the monarch physically signing each Commission had been stopped by an Act of 1862 which had been passed 'with a view to relieve her Majesty from the excessive labour of signing every separate commission for officers of the army, marines etc., ...'. In 1862 Her Majesty was still signing Commissions issued in 1858 and there were 15,931 waiting for signature when the Bill was passed. (Todd, pp. 336-7)

[14]Colonial Commissions here means those RCs issued directly from the British Government. There were numerous Vice-Regal Commissions set up by Governors-General in the name of the monarch which were appointed and operated in the same way as Royal Commissions, but which are not included in this volume. The choice of Royal or Vice-Regal Commission, especially in Irish matters, seems to have been as arbitrary as the distinction between Royal Commissions and Departmental Committees.

[15]These were issued under the Royal Sign Manual and Letters Patent respectively. There had been no Colonial Commissions since 1911, and it seems likely that following the upheavals of the War and the economic stringencies of the 1920s the relevant precedents had been either lost or forgotten. For an example of the difficulty of tracing precedents see the documents relating to the appointment of the Technical Sub-Committee of the Committee of Imperial Defence in 1926. (PRO.HO. 45/12477/496593)

[16]For example the Warrant for the RC into Grocers' Licences (no. **24**) begins: 'The Queen has been pleased to direct Letters Patent to be passed under the Seal appointed by the Treaty of Union to be kept and made use of in place of the Great Seal of Scotland appointing...'. Here again, there was a change after World War I, with the RC into the Court of Session (no. **189**) being issued under RSM and countersealed, and signed by J.C. Strettell Miller (Director of Chancery and Depute Keeper of the Seal); while the RC into

seemed to have been little coherent policy involved in the choice of instrument of appointment. From 1870 there does seem to have been a more consistent procedure although the reasoning behind it is obscure. Treasury and Home Office files often refer to notes on how to appoint Royal Commissions which were passed between different departments with the injunction, from the writers of various memoranda, 'Please return when done with'. It seems logical to assume that they rarely were returned, and officials generally relied on hazily remembered precedents when drawing up Warrants.[17]

The appointment of Royal Commissions was recorded in the *London Gazette* which published the Warrants in full and gave details of those Commissions appointed under Letters Patent. This remains the only complete official public record, although in most cases the full details were reprinted within the reports of the Commission. They are also preserved in the Home Office Warrant Books[18] and the Patent Rolls.[19] In the few cases where the Warrants were not reprinted, the omission seems to have been accidental rather than deliberate. However, in 1925 following a complaint from Lord Farrer[20] regarding what he saw as the needless inclusion of the Warrant in the ninth report of the Royal Commission on Ancient and Historical Monuments, Treasury officials referred the question to the Stationery Office who replied that 'There is apparently no Statutory obligation to insert the Royal Warrants of Appointment in the Reports of Royal Commissions'.[21] The letter went on to explain that there had been some correspondence with the Home Department regarding the procedure for semi-permanent Commissions such as Fine Art and Historical Monuments and that the Home Secretary had decided that their Warrants need only be included in their final reports and that 'It might be suggested to the Home Office that this procedure should in future be adopted in the case of all Royal Commissions, and an instruction to this effect might be incorporated in the

---

Licensing (no. **201**) was issued by Letters Patent without being countersealed, and was signed by the Scottish Secretary, William Adamson. In this case it seems most likely that the previous practice had been reversed.

[17]They sometimes resorted to academic texts. In 1926 Mr Leadbetter of the Treasury asked for Home Office help in drafting a Warrant of appointment for a technical sub-committee of the Committee of Imperial Defence, and was referred to Lowde's [*sic*] *Government of England* (possibly a reference to S.J. Low, *The Governance of England* (1914)). (PRO.HO.45/12477/496593)

[18]PRO.HO.38.

[19]PRO.C.66.

[20]Letter of 7 Dec 1925 to Treasury, in PRO.T.160/240/F.9074.

[21]Stationery Office to Treasury, 1 Jan 1926, as above.

"Instructions to Secretaries of Commissions and Committees".'[22]    It was proposed to the Home Office that a list of Commissioners and a brief summary of their duties and powers should be substituted for the full Warrant, but A.J. Eagleston, replying for the Secretary of State, rejected any changes in the established procedure except in those cases which the Home Office considered suitable.  Unusually the Treasury felt obliged to accept this.

        Such exchanges over the activities of Commissions were common throughout the period, as both Treasury and Home Office tried to order matters according to their own criteria of control.  The costs of staffing and housing Commissions were met from the Vote for Temporary Commissions, administered by the Treasury,[23] and although Commissioners were not paid,[24] they did receive expenses when their business took them away from home, and if overseas visits were required, the amounts could be large.  The Treasury often insisted that terms of reference should be worded so as to ensure that Commissioners took account of the financial implications of any recommendations they were asked to make; and the need for domestic Commissions to make foreign inquiries was always questioned.  Where there was a possibility that a Commission might want or need to go abroad Home Office practice was to try to insert the relevant clause into the original Warrant, since this avoided the need to obtain Treasury sanction

---

[22]These had been in use by the Treasury since at least 1870 (see Memo by R. Ferguson, n. 6), and by the Home Office since 1910 (see n. 11).  Various copies of these, showing successive revisions, are included in the PRO files;  see, for example, T.160/636/F2807.

[23]This was the case for all domestic Commissions, except the RC into the River Clyde (no. 13) whose costs were met by local authorities;  the costs of Colonial and Imperial Commissions were either met wholly by the relevant Department or shared between it and the Treasury.  However it should be noted that it has not been possible to check costs in all cases since there were no Parliamentary Returns of RC Costs after 1913 (PP. (159), li, 765), and the Treasury requirement that estimated costs be recorded on the Commission reports did not come into force until 1921.

[24]Exceptions were made in the case of Commissioners who were wage-earners and unable to work due to commission business.   There are also some examples where Commissioners made claims for loss of professional earnings, but payment of these was often resisted on the grounds that (a) the scale of allowable expenses took this into account, and (b) the honour attached to Commission work was its own reward.  See, for example, Treasury *Instructions for Secretaries*, and correspondence concerning Commissioners' and witnesses' expenses in PRO.T.160/636/2807;  T.160/49/E3730; HO.45/9330/19461A, and HO.45/9892/B17500.

at a later date.[25]  The Warrants had a standard form of words which described the duties of the Commissioners, and if it was intended that they should pursue their inquiries abroad the wording was changed accordingly.

Treasury officials attempted to control Commissions from their initial stages, and expected to be consulted about both appointees and terms of reference before the Warrants were drawn up.  The surviving Home Department files for the 1870-1900 period contain a number of instances where Warrants had to be amended following Treasury intervention, although there never seem to have been any objections to the choice of actual Commissioners.  However during and just after the war years the practice of submitting Warrants seems to have lapsed or (understandably) Treasury oversight was less keen.  A memorandum by B.P. Blackett states: 'I am to observe that this was formerly the normal practice, but it has not been invariably followed in recent years.'[26]

The form of the Warrant also had some implications for the appointment and responsibilities of Secretaries.  The practice of naming them in Warrants almost ceased after 1910,[27] and although, as Collinge has noted,[28] their inclusion in Warrants is apparently arbitary, it did in some cases affect their legal position in disputes between the Home Office and the Commission.  In the case of the inquiry into the premature publication of the evidence of the Commission into the Irish Land Acts (no. **97**), the Home Office rejected the suggestion that the Irish government should make inquiry of the Secretary, Richard Cherry.  It was pointed out that as he was named in the Warrant and that this was countersigned by the Home Secretary he was answerable to the Home Office and not the Irish government, thus his inclusion in the Warrant may have given him some protection in the inquiry.  However it was made clear to Cherry and to other Secretaries in similar situations that they were responsible for ensuring confidentiality in the affairs of the Commission, even though it was equally accepted that they had little control over the actions of Commissioners.  Following an earlier case in which the final report of the Commission on Vaccination had been published before its presentation to the Queen and

---

[25]The Commission on the Depression of Trade provides an instance of this: Home Office memoranda note the need for a clause authorising overseas visits, but following Treasury scrutiny of the draft Warrant this was omitted. (PRO.HO.45/9656/A40724)

[26]PRO.T.160/93/F.3307, May 1921.

[27]The Departmental Committee into Procedure of Royal Commissions (1910, Cd.5235, lviii, 371) had recommended the omission of the Secretary's name from the Warrants, and thereafter the names were usually only included on Commissions dealing with Colonial or Imperial matters.

[28]*Officials 1815-70*, p. 6.

Parliament,[29] it had been decided to reinforce the Letter of Instructions to Secretaries of Commissions and Committees which accompanied their Warrant or letter of appointment by sending a further letter when the report was nearing completion. Copies of the re-drafted letters are included in the file of correspondence relating to the Royal Commission on South African Hospitals (no. **105**), but it is not clear how soon they came into use. From this time it seems to have been the practice to send a printed form of acknowledgement to the Secretary when he had submitted a report, which specifically forbade its contents being divulged 'until you have satisfied yourself by enquiry at the Vote Office of the House of Commons or at the Stationery Office that the document has been distributed to the members of both Houses of Parliament'.[30]

It was established protocol that the signed report was submitted to the monarch by the Home Secretary, and subsequently presented to the House, although the practice for submitting evidence was less clear, and may have resulted in some of the premature publication complained of by Members of Parliament and Home Office officials. The report presented to Parliament was often a dummy (i.e. a front cover only),[31] while the actual report was submitted to the monarch. In very rare instances a dummy was sent to the monarch, when approval was needed urgently in order that a report could be presented to Parliament before the end of a Session, but it was noted by Sir Godfrey Lushington (9 Aug 1888) that this was irregular.[32] However, much of the work of Commissions consisted of collecting and hearing evidence and this was usually presented before the substantial report with the Commission's recommendations. The convention was that volumes of evidence could not be presented without a report and Secretaries were evidently often unsure of the form such reports should take, sometimes reproducing the complete formal warrant with each volume of evidence and at other times submitting the evidence with only a

---

[29]A letter of 7 Oct 1896 to the Secretary, Bret Ince (who had not been named on the Warrants of appointment), described the leak as a 'grave impropriety'. (PRO.HO. 45/9810/B6619)

[30]This was included in the papers of the RC on South African Hospitals (no. **105**) and was sent to its Secretary, Major Tennant, on 18 Jan 1901. (PRO.HO.10201/B32430)

[31]PRO.HO.45/10201/B32430.

[32]This was the case with the second report of the RC into Civil Establishments (no. **59**) and the third report of the RC into Gold & Silver (no. **60**). See PRO.HO.45/9760/B.661.30 and HO.45/9665/A44765.

covering letter to the Secretary of State.[33] It was not until 1907 that an attempt was made to establish a uniform procedure for the submission of evidence when it was stated that the Commission required only the opinion of Commissioners to be submitted to the monarch; evidence could be published at their discretion whether or not accompaied by a report, as could reports of their proceedings which did not include opinions or recommendations. The usual practice of publishing evidence with only a cursory report being sent to the monarch was seen as disrespectful, and the Home Office *Instructions* were amended to allow Commissions to publish evidence without a formal report. Subsequent economies further circumscribed the publishing of evidence, which ceased to be printed as Command Papers after 1922, and was thereafter published as non-Parliamentary Papers.

Both the Home Office and the Treasury had adopted formal Instructions for the guidance of Commissions,[34] but Chairmen and Secretaries were often unclear about procedure as so many matters were governed by precedent rather than by fixed rules. This reflected the ambiguous position of the Commissions themselves, since they were bound by neither the increasingly regulated civil service administration (despite the best endeavours of the Treasury), nor the direct scrutiny of Parliament. Because of the traditional view that each Commission, once appointed, was an independent body, the Home Office resisted any requests from Secretaries for a definite ruling in their internal procedures, offering only references to previous cases, and leaving any decisions to the Commission.[35]

The Home Office was usually much clearer about the lines of communication between Commissions and Departments of State. In general all requests and enquiries from Commissions were dealt with by the Commission Secretary and the Permanent Under Secretary of State at the Home Office as Commission Secretaries and Chairmen were often forcefully reminded. The Marquess of Hartington, Chairman of the Labour Commission (no. **77**) wrote to

---

[33]Some Secretaries were unclear about the procedure for obtaining the Commissioners' signatures to the reports, erroneously believing that they had to assemble the whole Commission for a communal signing session (see PRO.HO.45/9925/B24578, RC on Irish Land Acts). Conversely, many of the surviving signed reports are excellent examples of cutting and pasting techniques which give rise to the suspicion that Secretaries often resorted to cutting Commissioners' signatures off other letters and sticking them to the report in order to save time (see for example PRO.HO.9869/B14051, report of the RC on Land in Wales).

[34]See n. 11 and n. 22.

[35]See, for example, no. **91**.

the Secretary of State[36] wanting to liaise with the appropriate Home Office official over the appointment of Assistant Commissioners, but was told that in such matters the Commission is 'always silent'. Various precedents were quoted where a Chairman had recommended names to the Secretary of State who then obtained Treasury approval for the appointments which were formally made by the Home Office. Matthews noted 'Let the course followed be in future that the Secretary of State shall appoint Assistant Commissioners, taking into account the recommendations of the chairman of the Commission'.[37]

The method of appointment of administrative staff was similar, although there were frequent variations in practice, largely due to the lack of knowledge of procedure by successive Secretaries and the inability or unwillingness of the Home Office to make and keep a standard set of guidelines. Commission staffs were always temporary[38] and as their composition was not determined in advance, they could be large, especially for those Commissions which took many volumes of oral evidence.[39] The bulk of the correspondence between their Secretaries, the Home Office and the Treasury consists of matters relating to the appointment of staff. The Treasury was less concerned about the protocol of communication in these matters than the Home Office: one Treasury official noted that the Home Office had failed to endorse a set of proposed salary increases for the Labour Commission and that this was not correct procedure, but continued 'I attach little importance to it. The opinion of the Home Office is not likely to help us about Temp. Comm. Establishments' (abbreviated in original).[40]

The key appointment of a Royal Commission was that of the Secretary; he[41] was expected to liaise and mediate between all the parties involved in the

---

[36]11 Apr 1891.

[37]PRO.HO.45.9837/B10296.

[38]The 1910 Departmental Committee (Cd.5235) had proposed a permanent staff for Commissions but this was not adopted.

[39]This was a practice which Commissions were very reluctant to give up. In 1921 an internal Treasury report on possible economies in the organisation of Commissions proposed that evidence should not be reported verbatim: the writer noted parenthetically, 'we always try and usually fail'. (S.D. Wiley, 17 May 1921, PRO.T.160/93/F.3307)

[40]Sir E. Hamilton, 12 Dec 1891, PRO.T.1/17733.

[41]All Secretaries to Royal Commissions which sat between 1870 and 1940 were male, as were the Chairmen. One woman, Audrey M. Fletcher was appointed Assistant Secretary to the Commission on Common Law 1934-36; the first woman to be appointed a full Secretary was Miss M. Dennehy who succeeded K.A.S. Edwards as Secretary to the RC

Commission, with responsibilities that ranged from advising Commissioners on legal and technical details to the ordering of stationery.[42] The Treasury's view of the role of the Secretary is made clear in the first paragraph of their *Instructions*:[43] he was a Sub-Accountant of the Treasury and as such was directly responsible for seeing that the *Instructions* were carried out. From the 1870s Secretaries were increasingly recruited from the higher ranks of the Civil Service, although outside appointments continued to be made.[44] Chairmen were given considerable power over the nomination of Secretaries and Assistant Secretaries and the post was seen as one of patronage.[45] This is demonstrated in the correspondence between the Treasury, the Board of Agriculture, the Home Department and Herbert Lyon regarding the appointment of an Assistant Secretary for the 1893 Commission on Agriculture (no. **86**). The Board of Agriculture proposed the appointment of Mr. R.F. Crawford and Sir R. Welby wrote to the Home Office to enquire if the Secretary of State would recommend the appointment to the Treasury. The reply from C. Deffell begins without preamble:

> The Dept. has nothing to do with the appointment of a Secretary or an Assistant Secretary to a Royal Commission unless the appointment is made by the Queen, in which case the Warrant of appointment is made up here, after the name of the appointee has been submitted to H.M. and approved.
> Frequently the appointment of a Secretary to a Royal Commission is a piece of patronage exercised by the Chairman, I believe, in which case neither the Queen nor the Secretary of State has anything to do with it.
> My answer to your note depends, therefore, upon how it is desired that Mr. Crawford should be appointed.
> It is quite unusual for the Queen to appoint an *Assistant* Secretary, but it could be done, if desired, no doubt.

The operation of patronage did not necessarily run counter to the practice of

---

on Divorce (1951-55, Cmd.9678).

[42]Secretaries frequently became very involved with their Commissions; for example, D.L. Thomas (Secretary to the RC on Wales, no. **83**) was instrumental in having the report translated into Welsh (PRO.HO.45/9869/B14051), while A.S. Charlton (Secretary to the RC on Tyneside, no. **21**) reminded Commissioners of their social obligations, suggesting that they write to the Chairman to congratulate him on his marriage (PRO.HLG.11/3). See also no. **47** on Liddell.

[43]See n. 22.

[44]Usually from the legal profession although occasionally academics were appointed: the Secretary to the 1920 Commission on Dublin University (no. **175**) was Gilbert Waterhouse, Professor of German at the University of Dublin.

[45]Some Chairmen appointed their own private secretaries or members of their families.

appointing civil servants since many Chairmen were or had been members of government or Ministers of State, and would thus already be acquainted with a range of suitable candidates from within the Civil Service.

Members of the Civil Service appointed as Secretaries and Assistant Secretaries were often seconded from their usual departments, and this could cause problems. The Treasury guidelines over payment were clear: if a person was already being paid from public funds they were to receive no extra payment for Commission work, apart from allowable expenses.[46] Thus the Treasury authorised a salary of £400 per annum for Geoffrey Drage, a barrister and one of the Joint Secretaries to the Labour Commission (no. **77**), while the other, John Burnett, Labour Correspondent of the Board of Trade, was paid a gratuity of £250 per annum because 'My Lords assume that Mr. Burnett will continue to perform his duties at the Board of Trade'.[47] The secondment of civil servants was not always cheaper than outside appointments, and the Treasury frequently sought reassurance from Departments that the person would be able to carry out their departmental duties in addition to the Commission work, and that the original Department would not put in a request for additional assistance.[48] Despite the Treasury *Instructions* there were still instances of confusion over the status of such secretaries.[49]

Although the *Instructions* were characteristically clear about payment there was considerable ambiguity, or as the Treasury preferred to put it 'discretion', over the matter of gratuities. In 1891 Geoffrey Drage, Secretary to the Labour Commission (no. **77**) requested a salary increase to give him £700 per annum; he was not granted the full amount but a file note by Sir E. Hamilton states that it should be intimated '(officially or privately) that when the work of the Commission is concluded we would be prepared to consider the question of a gratuity...'.[50] However when the Duke of Devonshire (Chairman of the Labour Commission) wrote requesting a gratuity of £500 for Drage, Sir J.

---

[46]It was also made clear that expenses claims were to be strictly demarcated both for Secretaries and also for Commissioners: Para. 29 of the Treasury *Instructions* states that during Parliamentary Sessions claims for London travelling expenses of Commissioners who are also MPs would be met only if the Member certified that his presence in London was solely in connection with Commission business. The *Instructions* further state that travelling expenses for Witnesses to Commissions were to be paid *'according to class in life'* (their italics).

[47]Treasury to HO, 29 June 1891, PRO.HO.45/9837/B.10296/4.

[48]RC on Loss of Ships, PRO.HO.45/9648/A37324; RC on Labour, cited above n. 47.

[49]See no. **75**, RC on Tithe Rent Charge.

[50]Note dated 11 Dec 1891, T.1/16971.

Hibbert refused to sanction this on the grounds that it was unprecedented.[51] In a later case[52] the Secretary to the Commission on Health Insurance (no. **184**), Edgar Hackforth, was similarly refused a gratuity, and it was suggested that a more suitable reward would be a C.B.E.

Administrative structures varied according to the size and terms of reference of the Commission, but in addition to the Secretary most Commissions employed at least one clerk and a messenger.[53] From 1870 staff below the level of Assistant Commissioner, Secretary, or Assistant Secretary were expected to show that they met the appropriate Civil Service qualifications for their post[54] if they did not already hold a relevant certificate of competence.[55] Some Commissions employed staff from outside firms, most notably shorthand writers, whose remuneration was also subject to Treasury controls.[56] As has been noted, there are many gaps in both Treasury and Home Office records for Commissions which means that it is impossible to do more than draw very tentative conclusions from those that survive. An examination of these does seem to indicate that while the Lords of the Treasury may have complained about the expenses of Commissions,[57] requests for staff were usually granted, albeit with

---

[51]Letter from Duke of Devonshire dated 26 June 1894; Sir J. Hibbert reply 20 July 1894 in PRO.T.1/8834B/10049.

[52]PRO.T.162/116/E15897. See also no. **47**.

[53]There were some instances of parallel employment, when two or more Commissions shared premises: the RC on Oxford & Cambridge (no. **4**) shared a Messenger with the RC on Friendly Societies (see *Officials 1815-70*, no. **135**).

[54]This practice was the result of a compromise between the Treasury and the Civil Service Commission and is detailed in R. Ferguson's 1877 Memorandum (see n. 6).

[55]Treasury *Instructions*, 1 May 1894, para. 2. (PRO.HO.45/9874/83324)

[56]PRO.T.160/196 contains correspondence regarding the employment of an outside firm by the RC on Lunacy (no. **185**) which the Treasury attempted to prevent by suggesting the use of clerks from their own pool. They were forced to concede that other demands on the pool, especially in the form of an Imperial Conference meant that they must 'let the Chairman of this Royal Commission have his way & employ Messrs. Gurney'. (O.E. Niemeyer, 9 Aug 1924)

[57]Following a number of requests from Herbert Lyon, Secretary to the 1894 Agriculture Commission, for additional Assistant Commissioners and extensions of employment for those already appointed, the Treasury wrote: 'My Lords must add that They are disappointed at the repeated failure of the Commission on Agriculture to confine the operations of the Assistant Commissioners within the limits originally estimated, and they trust that the present will be the last application for extension either of numbers or time'.

much haggling over rates of pay.[58]

Women had worked in clerical positions in the Civil Service since the 1870s, and were first employed on a Royal Commission in this capacity in the 1891-94 Labour Commission. These appointments were justified on grounds of economy rather than equity: Drage's submission for the employment of two Lady Clerks noted that he had the names of several 'ladies ... of high scholastic distinction at the Universities. ...It would be impossible to obtain men possessing such qualifications at the salary of £150 per annum, the lowest sum for which they will undertake the work'.[59] This Commission also employed the first female Assistant Commissioners, one of whom, May Abraham, subsequently became the first woman appointed as a British government factory inspector. However, neither she nor her colleagues on the Commission, whose terms of reference were to investigate the relations between employer and employed, seem to have been aware of the tensions on the Commission's own staff, which came to a head with the summary dismissal by Drage of one of the clerks, Miss Wilson.[60]

It had been proposed that women should be appointed as full Commissioners on the Labour Inquiry. James Bryce had put down a question to the Chancellor of the Exchequer[61] asking if women had been considered as members. Mr. W.H. Smith replied that the Government had come to the conclusion that this was not desirable and that 'All interests will doubtless be

---

Treasury to HO 16 June 1894. (PRO.HO.459875/B15063)

[58]The T.108 index gives many brief references to these, some of which are more fully recorded in the surviving T.1 files. In general Treasury practice was to accede to requests for additional staff in the hope (often misplaced) that Commissions would thereby be encouraged to complete their reports more quickly.

[59]Drage to Home Office, 7 Dec 1891, PRO.T.1/17733.

[60]Her father, A.J. Wilson, a journalist and editor of *The Investors' Review*, wrote and had privately printed a pamphlet, 'Lady Clerks and The Royal Commission on Labour' which reproduced correspondence between himself and Drage and detailed her grievances. He sent a copy to H.H. Asquith (Secretary of State for the Home Department) on 31 Oct 1892. The Home Department replied on 4 Nov 1892 that it had no power to interfere with either the Commission or with the conduct of any of its officials, and left the matter with Lord Hartington, the Commission's Chairman, who appears to have done nothing. (PRO.HO.45/9837/B10296)

[61]A protocol which underlines the formal reality of Treasury influence on such appointments.

fully represented before the Commission'.[62]   When Bryce was appointed Chairman of the Commission on Secondary Education in 1894 he may have been instrumental in the choice of three women as full Commissioners: Lady Lucy Cavendish, a former lady-in-waiting to Queen Victoria, and a leading philanthropist and supporter of women's education; Dr. Sophie Bryant, the first woman DSc of the University of London and Headmistress of the North London Collegiate School; and Mrs. Eleanor Sidgwick,[63] with her husband co-founder of Newnham College, Cambridge and its first Principal.[64]

        Appointments to Commissions reflected more general changes in ideas about political representation which accompanied the successive franchise reforms of the 19th and early 20th centuries.   The move towards appointing Commissioners to represent specific groups or sections of society changed perceptions of Commissions and their work.  The traditional view of a Royal Commission was as the embodiment of values rather than interests;  that the members were able to give impartial advice precisely because they were supposed to be above the sectionalism of political or social groupings.  Thus when Sir George Campbell in his minority report on the Fugitive Slaves Commission dissented from his colleagues on the question of how far legal obligations were outweighed by social and moral duties, he was speaking for a set of values which although they might affect the lives of fugitive slaves were not a representation of their views.  Neither Sir George nor his colleagues had ever been a fugitive slave, just as those Commissioners who reported on factory conditions had no experience of factory work, and such direct representation would not have been considered to be necessary or appropriate.  However in 1887 Thomas Knipe, a tenant farmer, and member of the Irish Land Laws Commission (no. **63**), refused to sign the majority report on the grounds that its principal recommendations were against the interests of the class he represented.[65]   Trades unionists and members of Trades Councils were appointed to Commissions during the last two decades of the 19th century,

---

[62]*Hansard*, 3rd Series, 16 March 1891, 1065-66.

[63]Both Mrs Sidgwick and Lady Lucy Cavendish were members of powerful political families; Eleanor Sidgwick was the sister of A.J. Balfour, for whom she acted as hostess before her marriage; while Lucy Cavendish was the niece of William and Catherine Gladstone, and the sister-in-law of the Duke of Devonshire.

[64]Women were named in the Warrants of appointment in terms of their marital status; thus Mrs Sidgwick was described as 'Eleanor Mildred, wife of Henry Sidgwick, Esquire, Doctor in Letters, Professor of Moral Philosophy in our University of Cambridge'.

[65]17 March 1887, C.5015, xxvi. Other Commissioners were equally concerned to stress their impartiality: see no. **187** on Warren, who emphasised that his duty as a Commissioner was 'wholly towards the public'.

although they were rarely men of very radical views.[66] From the early 20th century the representative nature of Commissions became more explicit, with some Warrants linking Commissioners to their sectional or national interests,[67] while members of others were acknowledged to have been chosen to represent particular organisations.[68] However neither Governments nor individual Departments favoured the universal application of representative principles: Alfred Mond (Minister of Health) summed up the case for a Royal Commission into London Government by insisting 'it is essential that no attempt should be made to have the various interests represented'.[69]

Most Commissioners continued to be chosen from a social or political elite, and were thus largely unafflicted by the class tensions that affected Knipe, and the changes in the nature of the Commissions were not reflected in a greater degree of dissent in their reports. Individuals and groups on Commissions produced minority reports or signed majority reports with reservations in much the same proportions throughout the period. The appointment of middle-class women[70] and working-class men was restricted to particular Commissions, and in general they continued to be dominated by lawyers, civil servants and businessmen, many of whom were also politicians.

---

[66]For example, Augustine Birrell QC wrote of Henry Broadhurst, a trades unionist MP and a member of the RCs on Reformatories (no. **47**), Housing (no. **54**), Market Rights (no. **65**) and Aged Poor (no. **82**), that 'the youthful Broadhurst would have made, had his lot been different, a first-rate public schoolboy'. In H. Broadhurst, *Henry Broadhurst MP: From a Stonemason's Bench to the Treasury Bench* (1901).

[67]For example the RCs on Natural Resources (no. **151**) and Local Government (no. **181**).

[68]RCs on Fire Brigades (no. **176**), Food Prices (no. **186**), and London Squares (no. **194**).

[69]Memo. LG45 to the Cabinet, 29 June 1921. (PRO.HLG.9/2/91002)

[70]Some women Commissioners came from working-class backgrounds; for example, Agnes Hardie and Florence Harrison Bell, both of whom were active in trades unionism and local politics and were married to Labour MPs (Mrs. Hardie subsequently became MP for Glasgow, Springburn, 1937-45).

# Lists of Commissions and Officials

## 1. King's Inns, Dublin 1870-72
App. 8 Aug 1870. Rep. 5 Feb 1872, C.486, xx, 739. Cost £335.
Viscount Monck; G.A. Hamilton (d. 17 Sept 1871); W.R. Le Fanu.
Secretary: M.J. Barry. (Barrister; named in Warr.)
**To inquire** into the total amount received by the King's Inns, Dublin on admission of attorneys and solicitors ... and the suitability of accommodation of members of the Incorporated Society of Attorneys and Solicitors of Ireland.

## 2. Supersession of Colonels 1871
App. 30 Jan 1871. Rep. 13 March 1871, House of Commons Paper no. 276, xxxix, 827. Costs met from Army funds.
Lord Cairns; Sir W.M. James; Sir G. Bramwell; Sir J. Yorke Scarlett; D.M. Stewart.
Secretary: J. Milton. (War Office; named in Warr.)
**To inquire** into and examine the recommendations made by the Select Committee to consider complaints of hardship on behalf of British Army Colonels, that an amalgamated list should be made of Colonels from British, Staff Corps and Indian local lists.
Yorke Scarlett signed the report but added a note of dissent.

## 3. Megaera 1871-72
App. 22 Nov 1871. Rep. 6 March 1872, C.507-i, xv. Cost £1,105.
Lord Lawrence; A. Brewster; Sir M. Seymour; Sir F. Arrow; H.C. Rothery; T. Chapman.
Secretary: G.P. Bidder. (Barrister; named in Warr.)
**To inquire** into the circumstances in which the ship *Megaera* was sent to Australia; the extent and cause of the leak and any other defects in her hull at the time she was beached at St. Paul's; the previous history of the ship and her classification at successive dates.
Rothery signed subject to a note of dissent.

## 4. Oxford and Cambridge 1872-73
App. 5 Jan 1872. Rep. 31 July 1874:1873, C.856-i-ii, xxxvii, Pt.I-Pt.III. Cost £1,654.
Duke of Cleveland; Lord F.C. Cavendish; Lord Clinton; Hon. J.W. Strutt; W.H. Bateson; B. Price; K.D. Hodgson.
Secretary: C.S. Roundell. (Named in Warr.)
The Heads of the Oxford Colleges had questioned the legality of the earlier (1850-52) Royal Commission*, and the issue of the 1872 Warrant was accompanied by a letter (24 Oct 1871) from Gladstone to the Vice Chancellors

of both Universities asking for permission to make the inquiry; this, and subsequent correspondence is printed with the report.

**To inquire** into the property and income belonging to, administered, or enjoyed by the Universities of Oxford and Cambridge and their Colleges and Halls, including prospects of increase or decrease of such property and income, and all matters of fact bearing on its state and circumstances.

The year of signature and publication of this report is given as 1874, although it is included in the sessional volume of the Parliamentary Papers for 1873, and was presented to Parliament on 4 Aug 1873. Treasury records show that members of the Commission's staff continued to be paid throughout 1874 (PRO.T.108/6/14298 and 7438) so it may be surmised that the documents presented in 1873 were the Commission's evidence, and that the collation of report and evidence in the sessional volume for 1873 took place some years later. A similar case occurred in the Commission on Indian Decentralisation of 1907 (no. **137**).

\* See Clokie & Robinson (1937), pp. 82-86.

### 5. Mauritius 1872-74
App. 17 Feb 1872. Rep. 5 Nov 1874: 1875, C.1115, xxxiv. Other papers: 1875, C.1115-i, xxxv; 1875, C.1188, liii, 201. Commissioners were paid and costs were met from colonial funds. (RSM&S)
W.E. Frere and V.A. Williamson.
Secretary: N.D. Davis. (Named in a separate Warr. of the same date.)
**To enquire** into the condition of the Indian labourers in the island of Mauritius.

### 6. Endowed Schools and Hospitals (Scotland) 1872-75
App. 12 Sept 1872. Rep. (1) 30 Apr 1873, C.755, xxvii; (2) 1 May 1874, C.976, xvii, 111; (3) 15 Feb 1875, C.1123-i-ii, xxix. Cost £2,724.
Sir T.E. Colebrooke; Earl of Rosebery; Sir W. Stirling-Maxwell; C.S. Parker; J. Ramsay; H.H. Lancaster; A.C. Sellar.
Secretary: S.S. Laurie. (Named in Warr.)
J.M.D. Meiklejohn was appointed Assistant Commissioner.
**To inquire** into all endowments of educational funds not reported on by the Commissioners under the Universities (Scotland) Act of 1858; and into the administration, and courses of study in any Hospitals or Schools supported by such endowments; and to recommend any necessary changes for the increase of their usefulness and efficiency.

### 7. Unseaworthy Ships 1873-74
App. 29 March 1873. Rep. (1) 22 Sept 1873, C.853-i, xxxvi, 315; (2) 1 July 1874, C.1027-i-iii, xxxiv. Cost £2,472.
Duke of Somerset; Duke of Edinburgh; Hon. H.G. Liddell; T.M. Gibson; Sir J. Hope; H.C. Rothery; A. Cohen; T. Brassey; P. Denny; G. Duncan; E.D. Edgell; C.W. Merrifield.
Secretary: F. Napier Broome.
**To inquire** into alleged unseaworthiness of British Registered ships from

overloading, deckloading, defective construction, condition, form, equipment, machinery, age, improper stowage and also the present system of Marine Insurance, state of law as to liability of shipowners for injury of their employees, and alleged practice of under-manning ships; and to suggest amendments to the law to remedy or lessen the above.

### 8. Legal Departments 1873-74
App. 3 Oct 1873. Rep. (1) 8 Dec 1873: 1874, C.949, xxiv, 557; (2) 30 July 1874, C.1107, xxiv, 583. Other papers: 1875, C.1245, xxx,163. Cost £2,010.
Lord Lisgar; Sir G.W.W. Bramwell; W. Law; G.O. Trevelyan; A. E. West; F. W. Rowsell.
Secretary: G.L. Ryder. (Named in Warr.)
To inquire into the Administrative Departments of the Courts of Justice, as recommended in the 2nd Report of the Select Committee of the House of Commons into expenditure for the Civil Services. The Commission was to investigate the numbers, salaries, superannuation and cost; administration; manner of appointment and promotion; to recommend who should be responsible for the organisation of the establishments and their relation to Treasury Commissioners. Also how to employ, or otherwise compensate, those formerly connected with the Courts of Justice on abolition of their judicial offices.
Bramwell did not sign the first report and published a minority report. The second report was signed by all the Commissioners, but a Supplementary Report was issued on 'Responsibility for Organisation of Establishments of Courts of Justice' signed by all members except Lisgar and Bramwell. Lisgar also published a Memorandum containing alternative proposals which was endorsed by Bramwell.

### 9. Army Officers 1873-74
App. 11 Oct 1873. Rep. 1 June 1874, C.1018, xii. Cost £320.
Sir W.M. James; Lord Penzance; G.W. Hunt.
Secretary: R.H. Knox.
To inquire into alleged grievances of some army officers as a consequence of the Act (34 & 35 Vict. c.86) for the abolition of purchase, sale or exchange of Commissions in the British Forces.

### 10. Labour Laws 1874-75
App. 19 March 1874. Rep. (1) 31 July 1874, C.1094, xxiv, 391; (2) 17 Feb 1875, C.1157-i, xxx. Cost £635.
Sir A.J.E. Cockburn; Lord Winmarleigh; E.P. Bouverie; R. Gurney; Sir M.E. Smith; J.A. Roebuck; T. Hughes; G. Goldney; A. Macdonald.
Secretary: F.H. Bacon. (Barrister; named in Warr.)
To inquire into the working of the Master and Servant Act 1867, and the Criminal Law Amendment Act (34 & 35 Vict. c.32), and whether any amendments or alterations were necessary. Also whether it was expedient to limit or define the law relating to conspiracy, either generally or as it affected the relation of masters and workmen.

Macdonald published a minority report.

**11. Railway Accidents 1874-77**
App. 8 June 1874. Rep. 2 Feb 1877, C.1637-i-ii, xlviii. Cost £4,633.
Duke of Buckingham & Chandos; Earl of Aberdeen; Earl de la Warr; Earl of
Belmore; Sir W.R.S.V. Fitz-Gerald; A.S. Ayrton; Sir J.L.A. Simmons; T.E.
Harrison; W. Galt.
Secretary: R. Anderson.
**To inquire** into the causes of railway accidents and the possibility of removing
them by legislation.
Harrison and Galt signed subject to reservations;  Galt's was particularly
extensive, covering ninety-nine points with two appendices.  Earl de la Warr did
not sign and wrote a separate report.
The Home Office files (PRO.HO.45/9364/34882) indicate that the report could
have been finalised in 1875, but was held up due to the absence of the Chairman
and Secretary who had left for India before it was signed.  Despite Home Office
assurance that it was believed to be 'usual in the absence of the Chairman the
Commissioner next named in the Commission takes the chair and acts as
Chairman' (Henry Selwin-Ibbetson [Under Secretary of State], replying to the
Secretary of the Commission on behalf of Home Secretary Sir Richard Assheton
Cross on 2 Nov 1875), the Commissioners appear to have decided to await the
return of the Duke of Buckingham before presenting their report.  This file also
contains notes regarding the order of precedence of peers on the Warrant
appointing the Commission; the order was decided according to the date of
creation of the title, thus Aberdeen (1682) precedes de la Warr (1761) and
Belmore (1797).

**12. Army Promotion 1874-76**
App. 7 Nov 1874. Rep. 5 Aug 1876, C.1569, xv, 77. Cost £656.
Lord Penzance; Lord Hampton; E.P. Bouverie; E.B. Johnson; A.J. Herbert; R.E.
Welby; C.J. Foster.
Secretary: T.D. Pigott. (Named in Warr.)
**To inquire** into matters of army promotion having reference to previous
enquiries and legislation on the subject and specifically to report on the rapidity
of promotion under the purchase system; how this might best be secured in the
future with justice to the officers of all ranks in those corps which were under
the purchase system; how adequate promotion of officers could be achieved in
order to maintain efficiency throughout the whole army; recommendations to
achieve justice in relations between Officers of British Forces and those of the
Indian Staff Corps.

**13. Pollution of the River Clyde 1874-76**
App. 15 Dec 1874. Rep. 21 March 1876, C.1464, xxxviii. Costs defrayed by local
authorities.
Sir J. Hackshaw.
Secretary: J.B. Nicolson. (Named in Warr.)

To inquire into what towns and places contributed to pollution of the River Clyde and its tributaries; how the sewage and refuse from such places could be got rid of without risk to public health or to the disadvantage of manufacture; and the best means of purification of the river.

## 14. Factory and Workshop Acts 1875-76
App. 25 March 1875. Rep. 10 Feb 1876, C.1443-i, xxix, xxx. Cost £2,288.
Sir J. Fergusson; Lord F.C. Cavendish; Lord Balfour of Burleigh; Sir C. Du Cane; H.R. Brand; T. Knowles; C.O. O'Conor.
Secretary: Sir G. Young.
To inquire into the working of the Factory and Workshop Acts with a view to their consolidation and amendment, especially whether they could be made more consistent and harmonious and their provisions extended to other industries, trades and occupations not previously included; whether further provisions were needed for the health and education of young persons and children.
Brand signed the report subject to a note of dissent. O'Conor did not sign and published a separate report objecting to the labour restrictions recommended by the Commission.

## 15. Spontaneous Combustion in Ships 1875-76
App. 2 Apr 1875. Rep. 18 July 1876, C.1586, xli. Cost £1,615.
H.C.E. Childers; Sir G. Elliot; H.H. Vivian; F.A. Abel; R. Cory; G. Duncan; J. Fenwick; J. Ferguson; C. Icely; J. Percy; W. Young.
Secretary: J.M. Carmichael. (Clerk to the Admiralty.)
To inquire into causes of spontaneous combustion in ships and remedies for their prevention.
All members signed the report but Abel and Percy appended a separate paper.

## 16. Vivisection 1875-76
App. 22 June 1875. Rep. 8 Jan 1876, C.1397-i, xli, 277; Index: 1877, C.1864, xxvii, 663. Cost £869.
Viscount Cardwell; Lord Winmarleigh; W.E. Forster; Sir J.B. Karslake; T.H. Huxley; J.E. Erichsen; R.H. Hutton.
Secretary: N. Baker. (Barrister; named in Warr.)
To inquire into the practice of subjecting live animals to experiments for scientific purposes, and to consider and report what measures, if any, it may be desirable to take in respect of any such practice. (In full.)
Hutton published an additional report.

## 17. Copyright 1875-78
App. 6 Oct 1875 and 17 Apr 1876. Rep. 24 May 1878, C.2036-i, xxiv, 163. Cost £1,617.
Earl Stanhope (d. 24 Dec 1875); Earl of Rosebery*; Hon. R. Bourke*; Sir C.L. Young; Sir H.T. Holland; Sir J. Rose; Sir H.D. Wolff; Sir L. Mallet; Sir J. Benedict; T.H. Farrer*; J.F. Stephen; F. Herschell; W. Smith ; H. Jenkins*; F.R. Daldy.

The Warrant naming this Commission was revoked following the death of Stanhope; the revised Commission of 17 Apr 1876 was chaired by Lord J.J.R. Manners and additionally appointed the Earl of Devon; E. Jenkins; J.A. Froude; and A. Trollope. Secretary: J. L. Goddard.

**To make inquiry** with regard to the laws and regulations relating to Home, Colonial and International Copyright. (In full.)

Only the Earl of Devon, Holland, Benedict, Herschell and Froude signed the report unconditionally; the other members (including the Chairman) attached a series of dissenting notes and/or reports. Mallet did not sign and appended a separate report.

* Those marked with an asterisk were not reappointed on 17 Apr 1876.

### 18. Fugitive Slaves 1876

App. 14 Feb 1876. Rep. 30 May 1876, C.1516-i, xxviii, 285. Cost £649.

Duke of Somerset; Sir A.J.E. Cockburn; Sir R.J. Phillimore; M. Bernard; Sir T.D. Archibald; Hon. A.H. Thesiger; Sir H.T. Holland; Sir L.G. Heath; Sir H.J.S. Maine; Sir G. Campbell; J.F. Stephen; H.C. Rothery.

Secretary: H. Howard.

**To inquire** into and upon the nature and extent of such international obligations as were applicable to questions as to the reception of fugitive slaves by British ships in territorial waters of foreign states; into instructions issued to ships' commanders; bearing of any engagements with other countries on such matters; and the relation of such instructions and engagements to the maintenance of rights of personal liberty by officers of ships; and steps to be taken to give them greater freedom of action in this respect.

Phillimore signed subject to a reservation. Campbell did not sign, and issued a minority report, dissenting from the Commission on the question of when legal obligations were outweighed by social and moral duties.

### 19. Municipal Corporations 1876-80

App. 17 Apr 1876. Rep. pres. 5 Feb 1880, C.2490-i, xxxi. Cost £3,614.

Sir M.E. Smith; Sir J.B. Karslake; Sir T.D. Archibald (d. 18 Oct 1876); W. Overend; J.L. Wharton.

Secretary: A.G.C. Liddell. (Barrister; named in Warr.)

A Warrant of 17 Nov 1876 appointed J.B. Maule to replace Archibald. S. Cave was appointed an additional Commissioner 10 May 1876.

**To inquire** into, and report on, the existing state of Municipal Corporations not subject to the Act (5 & 6 Will. IV c.76) providing for the regulation of Municipal Corporations in England and Wales and the acts amending this (other than the City of London); and generally in what manner it was expedient that Parliament should deal with such Corporations.

Karslake signed subject to a note of reservation.

### 20. Scottish Universities 1876-78

App. 24 Apr 1876; sealed in Edinburgh 4 May 1876. Rep. pres. 4 March 1878, C.1935-i-iii, xxxii-xxxv. Cost £2,248. (LPGS)

J. Inglis; Duke of Buccleuch & Queensberry; Lord Moncreiff; L. Playfair; Sir W.

Stirling-Maxwell (d. 15 Jan 1878); J. Craufurd (Lord Ardmillan; d. 7 Sept 1876); W. Watson; J. Muir; J.A. Froude; A.C. Swinton; T.H. Huxley; J.A. Campbell. Secretary: R. Berry. (Advocate and Professor of Law at Glasgow University; named in Warr.)

**To make diligent and full inquiry** into each of the Universities of Scotland: their Constitutions; administration; courses of study; examinations; appointments and conditions of academic staff; scholarships; financial position; and condition of buildings.

Dr Muir appended a note of reservation which he stressed was not a dissension from the main recommendations of the Commission, but concerned matters on which he had not made a definite judgement. Froude appended a number of suggestions concerning the Law and History School.

### 21. Noxious Vapours 1876-78

App. 18 July 1876. Rep. 13 Aug 1878, C.2159-i, xliv. Cost £1,884.

Lord Aberdare; Earl Percy; Viscount Midleton; Hon. W. Egerton; J.C. Stevenson; F.A. Abel; A.W. Williamson; H.E. Roscoe; W.W. Hornby. Secretary: G.A.R. FitzGerald. (Barrister; named in Warr.)

**To inquire** into the working and management of gas works and manufacturies from which vapours and gases are given off, to ascertain the effect produced thereby on animal and vegetable life, and to report on the means to be adopted for the prevention of injury thereto arising from the exhalations of such acids, vapours and gases.

Stevenson and Roscoe entered reservations to the final report.

### 22. Trinity College and Dublin University 1877-78

App. 15 March 1877. Rep. pres. 9 May 1878, C.2045, xxix, 59. Cost £546.

Earl of Belmore; M. Longfield; S.W. Flanagan; A.M. Porter; J.A. Galbraith; J. Mulholland. Secretary: H.B. Leech. (Named in Warr.)

The Warrant for this Commission was very long. The Commissioners were to inquire into administrative, teaching and financial matters relating to Trinity College consequent upon the passing of the Irish Church Act, 1869, and of the Dublin University Tests Act, 1873; their report to be made within twelve months of the date on the warrant. The Commission was subsequently extended for a further three months in a Warrant dated 11 Feb 1878.

Flanagan and Porter signed subject to a note of qualification.

### 23. London Stock Exchange 1877-78

App. 9 May 1877. Rep. 31 July 1878, C.2157-i, xix, 263. Cost £974.

Lord Penzance; Lord Blackburn; S.H. Walpole; E.P. Bouverie; Hon. E. Stanhope; Sir N.M. de Rothschild; H.H. Gibbs; B.B. Greene; J. Hollams; C.J. Kennard; S.R. Scott; J.R. Yorke. Secretary: R.G.C. Mowbray. (Barrister; named in Warr.)

**To inquire** into the origins, objects, present constitution, customs and usages of the London Stock Exchange, and the mode of transacting business there, whether

existing practices were in accordance with the law and requirements of public policy; and if not to advise how they might be beneficially altered.
Walpole, Stanhope, Greene and Scott signed subject to reservations.

### 24. Grocers' Licences (Scotland) 1877-78
App. 14 Aug 1877; sealed in Edinburgh 24 Aug 1877. Rep. pres. 8 March 1878, C.1941, xxvi. Cost £781. (LPGS)
Sir J. Fergusson; A.C. Swinton; P. M'Lagan; J.A. Crichton; W. Ferguson.
Secretary: W.J. Mure. (Named in Warr.)
**To inquire** into the laws regulating the sale and consumption of excisable liquors sold not for consumption on the premises in Scotland, and to report and recommend any alterations that might be needed in the law.

### 25. Extradition 1877-78
App. 18 Aug 1877. Rep. 30 May 1878, C.2039, xxiv, 903. Cost £664.
Sir A.J.E. Cockburn; Lord Selborne; Lord Blackburn; R. Gurney; Sir R. Baggallay; Sir W.B. Brett; Sir J. Rose; Sir J.F. Stephen; Sir W.G.G.V. Harcourt; W.T.M. Torrens.
Secretary: G.E. March. (Named in Warr.)
An additional Commission was issued on 3 Sept 1877 appointing the Hon. A.H. Thesiger.
**To inquire** into and consider the working and effect of the Law and Treaties relating to the Extradition of persons accused of crime. (In full.)
Torrens signed but added a note of dissent from Section VII.
(PRO.HO.45/9443/66843)

### 26. Penal Servitude Acts 1878-79
App. 17 Jan 1878. Rep. 14 July 1879: 1878-79, C.2368-i, xxxvii. Cost £1,629.
Earl of Kimberley; J.G. Talbot; C.O. O'Conor; S. Whitbread; W. Guy.
Secretary: E.R. Wodehouse. (Barrister; named in Warr.)
This Warrant was revoked and a new one issued on 12 Feb 1878, with the original names plus Sir H.T. Holland. An additional Warrant of 28 Feb 1878 appointed E.H. Greenhow to the Commission.
**To inquire** into the working of the Penal Servitude Acts. (In full.)
Guy signed subject to his appended memorandum.

### 27. Registration of Deeds, Ireland 1878-80
App. 22 Jan 1878. Rep. (1) 12 Aug 1879: 1878-79, C.2443, xxxi, 405; (2) 30 Oct 1880: 1881, C.2818, xxx, 349. Cost £2,046.
G.A.C. May; C. Palles; H.E. Chatterton; S.W. Flanagan; H. Ormsby; M. Longfield; F.W. Walsh; J.F. Elrington; C.H. Meldon; W. Findlater; C.O. O'Conor; D.H. Madden; R.O. Armstrong.
Secretary: R.J. Lane. (Named in Warr.)
Two further Commissions were issued: the first dated 1 March 1878 appointed C.W. Wilson to the Commission because of his particular knowledge of the Ordnance Survey of Ireland; he subsequently resigned and was replaced by C.N.

Martin in a Warrant dated 9 Jan 1880.
The Warrant cites previous acts regarding the registration of title in Ireland, and authorises the Commissioners that having regard to the changes in the system for England, they were **to enquire** into the system of registration and the claims of creditors on land and hereditaments in Ireland, and generally into the law relating to Judgments, Decrees, Orders, Crown Bonds, Recognizances, and Lis Pendens in Ireland, and whether any alterations and improvements needed to be made.
The Warrant also specified that the Commissioners must complete their enquiries within twelve months from the date of the Warrant, although this time limit was twice extended by Supplemental Commissions issued on 18 Jan 1879, and 24 March 1880. This and the inquiry into Trinity College (no. **22**) were the only Royal Commissions during this period which were subject to time constraints.
May, Palles and Meldon signed the first report subject to dissents. O'Conor did not sign it and also published a dissent. Flanagan was unable to attend any of the Commission's meetings and therefore did not sign. The second report was signed subject to dissenting observations by Meldon and O'Conor. Armstrong also attached observations to this report but stated that they were not a dissent. Longfield had attended only one meeting, and Flanagan again none, so neither signed.

### 28. Ecclesiastical Benefices 1878-80
App. 1 June 1878. Rep. 14 Aug 1879: 1878-79, C.2375, xx, 595. Other papers: 1880, C.2507, xviii, 373. Cost £865.
Duke of Cleveland; Lord G.H. Cavendish; Viscount Midleton; Bishop of Peterborough; Bishop of Ely; Sir W.M. James; Sir W.H. Stephenson; G. Cubitt; G. Venables.
Secretary: E.S. Hope; (Barrister; named in Warr.) subsequently became a Charity Commissioner and was succeeded 5 Feb 1879 by C.S. Wortley. (Also warranted.)
On 28 June 1878 a further Commission was issued appointing the Earl of Devon; Archdeacon Palmer and F.H. Jeune.
**To inquire** into the law and existing practice as to the sale, exchange and resignation of ecclesiastical benefices, and to recommend remedies for abuses if they are found to exist. (In full.)
The report was signed subject to reservations by the Earl of Devon, Viscount Midleton, James, Venables and Jeune.

### 29. City of London Charities 1878-80
App. 10 Aug 1878. Rep. 12 March 1880, C.2522-i-iii, xx. Cost £1,258.
Duke of Northumberland; R. Gregory; W. Rogers; F. Herschell; G. Cubitt; A. Pell; H.H. Gibbs.
Secretary: W.H. Birley. (Barrister; named in Warr.)
**To inquire** into and ascertain the rights of those persons who might have claims on various parochial charities in the City of London; and those who have been habitual recipients; and to make recommendations concerning the future administration of the charities.

Rogers and Herschell signed subject to separate memoranda; Pell signed subject to Herschell's memorandum, and added a further one of his own.

### 30. Indictable Offences 1878-79
App. 17 Aug 1878. Rep. pres. 16 June 1879*: 1878-9, C.2345, xx, 169. Cost £2,924.
Lord Blackburn; C.R. Barry; Sir R. Lush; Sir J.F. Stephen.
Secretary: H. Cowie. (Barrister; named in Warr.)
**To inquire** into and consider the provisions of a Draft Code relating to Indictable Offences prepared for the purpose of being submitted to Parliament during the ensuing session, and to report thereon, and to suggest such alterations and amendments in the existing law as might seem desirable and expedient.
The Commission initially investigated the situation only in relation to England, but later extended their inquiries to Ireland.
*The Parliamentary Papers contain a printing error for the date of signature of this report which is given as 12 June 1878; a letter from Cowie to Home Secretary Cross records that the report was sent to the Home Office on 13 June 1879, and it was presented to Parliament 16 June 1879. (PRO.HO.45/9552/63062B)

### 31. Endowed Institutions in Scotland 1878-81
App. 20 Aug 1878. Rep. (1) 1 Oct 1879: 1880, C.2493, xxiv, 459. An unnumbered report dated 15 Nov 1880, C.2768; (2) 30 Dec 1880, C.2790, 237; (3) 30 July 1881, C.3076, 1019. All in 1881: xxxvi. Cost £2,645.
Lord Moncreiff; Lord Balfour of Burleigh; Sir J. Watson; J. Ramsay; J.A. Campbell; P.G. Tait; J. Donaldson.
Secretary: G.R. Gillespie. (Advocate; named in Warr.)
The Commission was appointed to carry out the provisions of the Endowed Institutions (Scotland) Act, 1878 (41 & 42 Vict. c.48). The members were to hold office during Her Majesty's pleasure and were not to exceed seven in number. The Warrant also states that the Secretary should be paid.
The Commission inspected all of the relevant institutions and produced individual reports on each, all of which were included in the final reports.

### 32. Accidents in Mines 1879-81
App. 12 Feb 1879. Rep. (1) pres. 19 Aug 1881, C.3036, xxvi; (2) 15 March 1886, C.4699, xvi, 411. Cost £8,128.
W.W. Smyth; Sir George Elliot; F.A. Abel; J. Tyndall; T. Burt; R.B. Clifton; W.T. Lewis; L. Wood.
Secretary: A.J. Williams.
On 24 March 1879 Lord Lindsay (succ. as Earl of Crawford & Balcarres in 1880), was appointed as an additional Commissioner.
**To inquire** and report on accidents in mines and whether they could be prevented or limited by use of the scientific resources now available.
The delay between the appointment of the Commission and the publication of its final report was explained by the Commissioners as unavoidable because the experiments they had needed to conduct led to wider fields of enquiry which they had felt it was important to pursue.

### 33. Wellington College 1879-80
App. 20 June 1879. Rep. 14 July 1880, C.2650, xiii, 215. Cost £788.
Lord Penzance; Lord A.G. Russell; Bishop of Exeter; R. Lowe; G.T. Chesney.
Secretary: H.B. Deane. (Barrister; named in Warr.)
**To inquire** and report on the foundation, development and present condition of
Wellington College, an institution set up by subscription for the education of
orphan sons of officers in the Army and the former Army of the East India
Company.
The Commission's findings were not accepted by the Governors of the College
who had requested the appointment of a Royal Commission in the first place.
They appointed a further committee, chaired by Earl Cairns, to investigate what
they regarded as various errors of fact and in the interpretation of financial
statements in the Commission's report, and sent their report to the Home Office
on 24 March 1881. (PRO.HO.45/9578/83612)

### 34. Cathedral Churches 1879-85
App. 4 July 1879. Rep. (1) 8 Feb 1882, C.3141, xx, 13; (2) 20 Aug 1883,
C.3822, xxi, 15; (3) 23 March 1885: 1884-5, C.4371, xxi, 453. Cost £3,198.
1883, xxi and 1884-5, xxi also contain the reports for individual cathedrals, each
issued under a separate command number.
Archbishop of Canterbury (A.C. Tait: d. 1 Dec 1882); Viscount Cranbrook;
Bishop of Carlisle; Lord Coleridge; Sir H.M. Jackson; A.J.B. Beresford-Hope; C.
Dalrymple.
Secretary: Arthur Becher Ellicott. (Barrister; named in Warr.)
The Warrant was revoked and a new one issued 30 June 1880 appointing Lord
Blachford and Sir W.C. James (cr. Baron Northbourne, 5 Nov. 1884) to replace
Lord Coleridge who resigned.
**To inquire** into the condition of cathedral churches of England and Wales, and
the cathedral church of Christ Church, Oxford, and the duties of their members
and ministers and whether there was a need for further legislation. The
Commissioners were to produce a separate report for each cathedral, and were
to give each Dean and Chapter eight weeks' notice of their visit so that their
respective Dean and Canon might attend the meetings of the Commission with
the same authority as if they were named in the Warrant of appointment.
Cranbrook approved the final report, but did not sign it as he was out of the
country when it was completed. Tait's place on the Commission was taken by
his successor as Archbishop of Canterbury, E.W. Benson, formerly Bishop of
Truro.

### 35. Agricultural Interests 1879-82
App. 14 Aug 1879. Rep. (1)14 Jan 1881, C.2778-i, xv; (2) pres. 25 July 1882,
C.3309-i-ii, xiv. Other papers: 1880, C.2678, xxviii; 1881, C.2778-ii, C.2951,
xvi, C.3096, xvii; 1882, C.3375-i-vi, xv. Cost £24,226.
Duke of Richmond & Gordon; Duke of Buccleuch & Queensberry; Earl Spencer;
Lord Vernon; G.J. Goschen; Sir W.H. Stephenson; R.N.F. Kingscote; H. Chaplin;
J. Clay; J. Cowen; M. Henry; C. Howard; J.L. Naper; R. Paterson; B. Price; J.

Rice; C.T. Ritchie; B.B.H. Rodwell; W. Stratton; J. Wilson.
Secretary: W.A. Peel. (Named in Warr.)
An additional warrant of 4 June 1880 appointed Lord Carlingford and J. Stansfeld to the Commission. Goschen retired from the Commission on 7 May 1880 upon his appointment as Special Ambassador at Constantinople. Earl Spencer became Lord President of the Council and retired on 19 May 1880. Lord Carlingford retired 2 May 1881 when he became Lord Privy Seal; and Rice ceased to act as a Commissioner when he was appointed a Sub-Commissioner under the Land Law (Ireland) Act of 1881. The Commission appointed thirteen Assistant Commissioners who prepared regional and international reports: J. Coleman; S.B.L. Druce; A. Doyle; W.C. Little; G.J. Walker; J. Hope; Professor Baldwin; Major Robertson; J. Clay, Jnr; A. Pell; C.S. Read; H.M. Jenkins; C.L. Sutherland.
**To inquire** into the depressed condition of the agricultural interest, and the causes to which it was owing; whether those causes were of a permanent character, and how far they had been created or could be remedied by legislation. (In full.)
The Preliminary Report contained a Memorandum by Price. Carlingford, Stansfeld, Henry, Cowen, Clay and Rice did not sign the report and produced a separate one on the subject of Ireland. The final undated report contains supplementary memoranda by Lord Vernon, Stansfeld, Chaplin, Clay, Howard and Paterson. It also notes that the Commissioners had not received the assistance they were led to believe they could expect from the Assistant Commissioners for Ireland (Baldwin and Robertson).

### 36. Colonial Defences 1879-82

App. 8 Sept 1879. Rep. not pres. to Parliament, (1) 3 Sept 1881; (2) 23 March 1882; (3) 22 July 1882. Cost £3,492.
Earl of Carnarvon; H.C.E. Childers; Sir H.T. Holland; Sir A. Milne; Sir J.L.A. Simmons; Sir H. Barkly; T. Brassey; R.G.C. Hamilton.
In 1880 the Earl of Camperdown and S. Whitbread were appointed in place of Childers and Brassey who resigned as they had become ministers in the Gladstone administration. (PRO.CAB/7/7)
Secretary: Captain H. Jekyll. (Royal Corps of Engineers; named in Warr.) Asst. Sec: Lieutenant G.W. Bartram, app. 1880. (T.108/2214)
**To inquire** into the condition and sufficiency for the defence of the more important colonial sea-ports and of their coaling stations for the protection of commerce.
The third report was signed subject to additional remarks by Milne, Barkly and Hamilton, and an additional memorandum by Lord Carnarvon, Holland, Milne, Simmons and Barkly. The results of the inquiry were not made public; a letter from Lord Carnarvon to the Treasury (13 Jan 1883) confirmed that he no longer had any of the Commission's papers; that the limited number of copies of the report were in the keeping of the Secretary of State for the Colonies; and that the extremely confidential nature of the report and many of its annexed papers meant that it could not be treated as an ordinary Parliamentary paper. (PRO.T.1/14983/14995/83) Sir H.T. Holland's bound copies of the reports are

held at PRO.CAB/7-4. PRO.CAB/7/7 is the Commission's Minute Book.

### 37. Sewerage and Drainage in Dublin 1879-80
App. 9 Sept 1879. Rep. 19 June 1880, C.2605, xxx. Cost £805.
R. Rawlinson and F.X. MacCabe.
Secretary: W.J. Dixon. (Barrister; named in Warr.) A supplemental Commission was issued on 4 Nov 1879 replacing Dixon who had died with R. O'Brien Furlong. (Barrister.)
To inquire into the present system of sewerage and drainage in the city of Dublin, in so far as such sewerage and drainage affect the sanitary condition of the said city, and the state of the River Liffey flowing therein; and to inquire whether such system is directly or indirectly prejudicial to the public health, and whether any and what changes are necessary therein with a view to sanitary improvement. (In full.)

### 38. Landlord and Tenant (Ireland) Act 1880-81
App. 29 July 1880. Rep. 4 Jan 1881, C.2779, xviii. Cost £4,289.
Earl of Bessborough; R. Dowse; C.O. O'Conor; A.M. Kavanagh; W. Shaw.
Secretary: Sir G. Young. (Named in Warr.)
To inquire into and report on the working of the Landlord and Tenant (Ireland) Act 1870, and Acts amending the same.
O'Conor and Shaw signed subject to supplementary reports. Kavanagh did not sign and wrote a separate report.

### 39. City of London Livery Companies 1880-84
App. 29 July 1880. Rep. 28 May 1884, C.4073-i-iv, xxxix, Pts. I-V. Cost £2,775.
Earl of Derby; Duke of Bedford; Viscount Sherbrooke; Lord Coleridge; Sir R.A. Cross; Sir N.M. de Rothschild; Sir S.H. Waterlow; W.J.R. Cotton; A. Pell; W.H. James; J.F.B. Firth; T. Burt.
Secretary: H.D. Warr. (Barrister; named in Warr.)
To inquire into the circumstances and administration, and to report on desirable changes in the constitution and administration, of all companies named in the Second Report of the Commissioners appointed to inquire into Municipal Corporations in England and Wales.
Firth and Burt signed subject to separate memoranda and observations. A dissenting report was signed by Cross, Rothschild and Cotton, with a further Protest by Cotton both against the Majority Report generally and against specific points of the Dissenting Report.

### 40. Measurement of Tonnage 1880-81
App. 11 Oct 1880. Rep. 25 Aug 1881, C.3074-i, xlix. Other papers: 1882, C.3380, xxi, 645. Cost £1,921.
C.M. Norwood; Sir J. Stokes; Sir E.J. Reed; H.C. Rothery; T. Gray; J.P. Corry; R. Capper; J. Glover; T.D. Hornby; W. Pearce; T.B. Royden; B. Waymouth.
Secretary: J.E. Wilkins.
To inquire into and report on the present law for the measurement of tonnage;

and whether any changes were necessary having regard to just principles of taxation; the furtherance of trade; international arrangements; and, above all, safety.

Stokes signed but attached a note to the report pointing out what he believed to be certain misapprehensions on the part of Rothery and Glover. The latter, and Waymouth, did not sign, appending their reasons.

### 41. Inland Navigation (Ireland) 1880-82

App. 18 Oct 1880. Rep. 8 Feb 1882, C.3173-i, xxi, 101. Cost £1,254.

Viscount Monck; Lord Monteagle of Brandon; C.H. Dickens; J.P. Nolan; A.L. Tottenham; T.A. Dickson; J.B. Greene; J. Mulholland.

Secretary: D. Godley. (Named in Warr.)

To inquire respecting the system of Navigation which connected Coleraine, Belfast and Limerick and to report on its continued viability as a joint navigation and drainage system.

Dickens signed the report but attached a dissent.

### 42. Transvaal 1881-82

App. 5 Apr 1881. Rep. pres. 7 Feb 1882, C.3114, C.3219, xxviii, 493. Cost £14,155. (RSM&S)

Sir H.G.R. Robinson; Sir H.E. Wood; Sir J.H. De Villiers.

Secretary: St. L.A. Herbert.

W.B. Gurdon was appointed Assistant Commissioner for Finance.

To inquire into, and report on all matters relating to the future settlement of the Transvaal Territory, and to execute documents, and perform acts in connection therewith.

The Commission included detailed instructions from the Earl of Kimberley (Secretary of State for the Colonies). The Commissioners had wide powers and on 3 Aug 1881 executed a convention with the representatives of the Transvaal burghers (S.J.P. Kruger, M.W. Pretorius and P.J. Joubert), granting self-government to the inhabitants of the Transvaal in accordance with the principles and conditions expressed in the Commission's report.

Sir E. Wood signed a dissent to the report, but concurred generally with his colleagues.

### 43. Medical Degrees 1881-82

App. 30 Apr 1881. Rep. pres. 22 June 1882, C.3259-i, xxix, 489. Cost £1,948.

Earl of Camperdown; Bishop of Peterborough; W.H.F. Cogan; Sir G. Jessel; G. Sclater-Booth; Sir W. Jenner; J. Simon; T.H. Huxley; R. McDonnell; W. Turner; J. Bryce.

Secretary: J. White. (Barrister, named in Warr.)

To inquire into the grant of medical degrees and other diplomas; and the courses of education necessary to acquire the skill and knowledge to attain them; and also to inquire into conditions for registration as medical practitioners; and into the result of the Medical Act of 1858 and its amendments.

The Bishop of Peterborough, Sclater-Booth, Simon, Huxley, Turner and Bryce dissented to parts of the report, and gave their opinions in a series of attached memoranda.

## 44. Ecclesiastical Courts 1881-83

App. 16 May 1881. Rep. pres. 14 Aug 1883, C.3760-i, xxiv. Cost £2,692.
Archbishop of Canterbury (A.C. Tait: d. 1 Dec 1882); Archbishop of York*; Marquess of Bath; Earl of Devon*; Earl of Chichester*; Bishop of Winchester*; Bishop of Oxford*; Bishop of Truro (subsq. Archbishop of Canterbury); Lord Penzance; Lord Blachford; Lord Coleridge*; Sir R.J. Phillimore*; Sir R.A. Cross; Sir W.C. James*; W.C. Lake*; J.J.S. Perowne*; B.F. Westcott; W. Stubbs; J.P. Deane*; E.A. Freeman*; T.E. Espin*; A.C. Ainslie; A. Charles; F.H. Jeune*; S. Whitbread.
Secretary: A.B. Kempe. (Barrister; named in Warr.)
**To inquire** into the constitution and working of the Ecclesiastical Courts, as created or modified under the Reformation Statutes of the 24th and 25th years of Henry VIII and any subsequent acts. (In full.)
* Signed the report subject to reservations. Lord Penzance did not sign and wrote a separate report.

## 45. Technical Instruction Abroad 1881-84

App. 25 Aug 1881. Rep. (1) 17 Feb 1882, C.3171, xxvii, 653; (2) 4 Apr 1884, C.3981-i-iii, xxix-xxxi(1). Cost £2,605.
B. Samuelson; H.E. Roscoe; P. Magnus; J. Slagg; S. Smith; W. Woodall.
Secretary: G. Redgrave. (Named in Warr.)
**To inquire** into the instruction of the industrial classes of certain foreign countries in technical and other subjects, to compare them with corresponding classes in this country; and into the influence of such instruction on manufacturing and other industries at home and abroad.
The second report records the appointment of H.M. Jenkins as sub-commissioner. The Commission's foreign visits gave rise to Treasury suspicions: an entry in the T.108 index for 1882 notes 'Comm. wants sharply looking after. Members have been taking a holiday at public expense'. (Entry no. 15762 - the file itself has been destroyed.)
PRO.HO.45/9612/A8064 has correspondence regarding the appointment of the Commissioners.

## 46. Smallpox Hospitals 1881-82

App. 16 Nov 1881. Rep. 21 July 1882, C.3314, xxix. Cost £871.
Lord Blachford; Sir J. Paget; Sir R. Alcock; A.W. Peel; E.L. Pemberton; J.B. Sanderson; A. Carpenter; W.H. Broadbent; J. Hutchinson.
Secretary: N. Baker. (Barrister; named in Warr.)
**To inquire** into the provision of hospital accommodation for smallpox and fever patients in the Metropolis, and to make any necessary suggestions for its improvement.

## 47. Reformatories & Industrial Schools 1882-84

App. 1 March 1882. Rep. pres. 5 Feb 1884, C.3876-i, xlv. Cost £2,234.
Lord Aberdare; Earl of Dalhousie; Lord Norton; Hon. E. Stanhope; Sir M.E.

Hicks-Beach; C.O. O'Conor; Sir U.J. Kay-Shuttleworth; D.La T. Colthurst; G. Woodyatt-Hastings; F.H.N. Glossop; C. Dalrymple; H. Broadhurst; W. Ewart; W.E. Hubbard, Jnr.
Secretary: A.G.C. Liddell. (Barrister; named in Warr.)
**To inquire** into and report upon the operation, management, control, inspection, financial arrangements and condition generally of Certified Reformatories, Certified Industrial Schools and Certified Day Industrial Schools in the United Kingdom; and to suggest any amendments to increase their efficiency.
Dalhousie, Norton, Broadhurst and Glossop signed the report, but attached memoranda expressing reservations.
Liddell resigned 28 July 1883 as he had taken up the post of Revising Barrister for the West Riding of York and could no longer hold an office of profit under the Crown. However he informed the Home Office that he wished to continue as unpaid Secretary to the Commission until its report was completed. In addition to this work he prepared a detailed memorandum setting out the Commission's recommendations and suggesting means by which they could be incorporated in legislation. There is no record of Treasury sanction for the out-of-pocket expenses he had also requested, but a file note of 7 Dec 1883 records that he was to be sent a 'very civil letter of thanks'. (PRO.HO.45/9617/A.13312)

**48. Metropolitan Sewage 1882-84**
App. 22 June 1882. Rep. (1) 31 Jan 1884, C.3842-i, xli; (2) 27 Nov 1884: 1884-5, C.4253-i, xxxi, 341. Cost £2,735.
Lord Bramwell; Sir J. Coode; A.W. Williamson; F.S.B.F. de Chaumont; T. Stevenson; J. Abernethy.
Secretary: W. Pole. (Named in Warr.)
A supplementary Commission was issued on 1 Nov 1882 appointing Sir P.B. Maxwell and C.B. Ewart.
**To inquire** and report upon the system under which sewage is discharged into the Thames by the Metropolitan Board of Works, whether any evil effects result therefrom, and in that case what measures can be applied for remedying or preventing the same. (In full.)
Benson Maxwell attached a letter to the first report stating his agreement with it. He was unable sign it due to his absence from England on public duty in Egypt. Coode was out of the country when the final report was signed but authorised the Secretary to sign for him.

**49. Educational Endowments (Scotland) Act 1882-89**
App. 26 Aug 1882. Rep. 31 Dec annually 1883-89 (1) 1884, C.3995, xxvii; (2) 1884-5, C.4329, xxvii; (3) 1886, C.4664, xxviii; (4) 1887, C.4981, xxxiii; (5) 1888, C.5312, xli, 841; (6) 1889, C.5641, xxxii, 569; (7) 1890, C.5957, xxxi, 763. Cost £14,429.
Lord Balfour of Burleigh; Earl of Elgin; Sir T.J. Boyd; Lord Shand; J.A. Campbell; J. Ramsay; J. Ure.
Secretary: A. Gibson (d. 1887). (Named in Warr.)
Like the Moncreiff Commission (no. **39**) this was a semi-permanent Commission

set up under the provisions of the Educational Endowments (Scotland) Act.

### 50. West Indian Finance 1882-83
App. 9 Dec 1882. Rep. pres. in 2 parts: 5 Feb and 4 Apr 1884, C.3840-i-iii, xlvi. Costs met by colonial funds. (RSM&S)
W. Crossman and G.S. Baden-Powell.
Secretary: C.A. Harris. (Named in Warr.)
**To inquire** into the public revenues, expenditure, debts and liabilities of the islands of Jamaica, Grenada, St. Vincent, Tobago and St. Lucia, and the Leeward Islands.

### 51. Irish Prisons 1882-83
App. 29 Dec 1882. Rep. (1) 3 Feb 1883, C.3496, xxxii, 803; (2) 1 Aug 1884: 1884-5, C.4233-i, xxxviii. The second report was also published separately as 1884, C.4145, xlii, 671. Cost £2,360.
Sir R.A. Cross; Hon. W. St. J.F. Brodrick; E.R. Wodehouse; R. McDonnell; G. Sigerson; N.D. Murphy; T.A. Dickson.
Secretary: A.B. McHardy. (Major in Royal Engineer Corps; named in Warr.)
**To inquire** into the administration, discipline and condition of local and convict prisons in Ireland.

### 52. Crofters and Cottars in Highlands and Islands of Scotland 1883-84 App.
17 March 1883, and sealed in Edinburgh 22 March 1883. Rep. pres. 4 Apr 1884, C.3980, xxxii. Other papers: C3980-i-iv, in vols. xxxiii-vi. Cost £5,961. (LPGS)
Lord Napier; Sir K.S. Mackenzie; D. Cameron; C. Fraser-Mackintosh; A. Nicolson; D. MacKinnon.
Secretary: Malcolm M'Neill. (Named in Warr.)
**To inquire** into the condition of the crofters and cottars in the Highlands and Islands of Scotland.
Mackenzie, Cameron and Fraser-Mackintosh attached reservations to the main report.

### 53. Trawling 1883-85
App. 30 Aug 1883. Rep. pres. 9 March 1885: 1884-5, C.4328, xvi, 471. Cost £1,766.
Earl of Dalhousie; Hon. E. Marjoribanks; T.H. Huxley; W.S. Caine; T.F. Brady.
Secretary: A.G.C. Liddell.
**To inquire** into the complaints of line and drift-net fishermen owing to the use of the trawl-net and beam trawl in the Territorial waters of the United Kingdom, whether such complaints were well founded and whether any, and what, legislative remedy could be adopted without interfering with the cheap and plentiful supply of fish.
Professor Huxley did not sign the report and had been unable to attend the later sessions of the Commission because of illness.

**54. Housing of the Working Classes 1884-85**

App. 4 March 1884. Rep. (1) pres. 7 May 1885: 1884-5, C.4402-i-ii, xxx; (2) pres. 14 May 1885, C.4409-i (Scotland), xxxi; (3) pres. 4 Aug 1885, C.4547-i-iii (Ireland), xxxi. Cost £2,377.

Sir C.W. Dilke; Prince of Wales; Cardinal Archbishop Manning; Marquess of Salisbury; Earl Brownlow; Lord Carrington; G.J. Goschen; Sir R.A. Cross; Bishop Suffragan of Bedford; Hon. E.L. Stanley; W.T.M. Torrens; H. Broadhurst; J. Collings; G. Godwin; S. Morley.

Secretary: J.E.C. Bodley. (Barrister; named in Warr.)

A supplementary Commission of 16 Aug 1884 appointed Sir G. Harrison and E.D. Gray.

**To inquire** into the housing of the working classes. (In full.)

The drawing up of the Warrant for this Commission raised some difficult matters of protocol since it involved the appointment of Manning who was not only a Roman Catholic archbishop but 'a Cardinal Prince of a State which we do not recognise' (Harcourt [Secretary of State] to the Lord Chancellor [the Earl of Selborne], 26 Feb 1884). According to this correspondence no-one had thought of the difficulties this would produce. There were precedents for the appointment of Roman Catholic Archbishops in both the Royal Commission upon Charitable Donations of 1844 and the Royal Charter of the University of Ireland, where they took precedence over Earls but not Archbishops of the Church of England, but no record could be found of the appointment of a Cardinal. It was resolved that Manning should rank next after the Prince of Wales, whose agreement to this was noted, but that there should be no 'distinctive epithets such as "Eminence" nor any allusion to the territorial titles of his See'. It was also necessary for the Home Office to obtain a legal opinion as to the rank and precedence of Suffragan Bishops relative to the appointment of Bishop Walsham. The Law Officers ruled (8 March 1884) that 'We are of opinion that Suffragan Bishops appointed under the Act of Henry VIII are not by virtue of their offices, entitled to any precedence outside their dioceses ...'. (PRO.HO.45/9641/A34692)

All signed the first report: Salisbury, Goschen and Cross subject to reservations. A supplementary report was signed by Manning, Carrington, Harrison, Stanley, Gray, Torrens, Broadhurst, Collings, Godwin and Morley. A number of individual and joint memoranda were produced, with various combinations of Commissioners expressing support for some or all of the views expressed in them. Jesse Collings did not sign the second report and attached a memorandum explaining his reasons. This was also signed by Dwyer Gray and Broadhurst, although they had signed the main report. All Commissioners signed the third report: Cross, Brownlow, Dwyer Gray and Collings subject to reservations.

**55. Loss of Life at Sea 1884-87**

App. 1 Nov 1884. Rep. (1) 31 July 1885: 1884-5, C.4577, xxxv; (2) 27 Aug 1887, C.5227-i-ii, xliii. Cost £3,538.

Earl of Aberdeen; Duke of Edinburgh; J. Chamberlain; Sir C.P. Butt; J.E. Gorst (ktd. 1885); T.C. Baring; T. Burt; H. Green; J. Kennedy; J. McGregor; W. Pearce; L.D. Smith; L.C. Wakefield; W. Walton.

Secretary: R. Anderson. (Barrister; named in Warr.)

A Commission of 20 Dec 1884 appointed E. Heneage, J. Aste, G.A. Laws, H.W. Parker, T.B. Royden and J. Warrack.

The first Commission was revoked and a new one issued on 4 March 1884 naming Sir A.C. Key in addition to those members appointed under the previous Warrants. The terms of the Warrant remained the same.

**To inquire** into the extent and cause of loss of ships and lives at sea since the report of the Commission on Unseaworthy Ships; and to report on remedies especially laws regarding insurance and liability; the functions and administration of the Marine Department of the Board of Trade, and of Courts dealing with Wreck Inquiries; and the condition and efficiency of Merchant Officers and Seamen.

Royden, Green, Watson Parker and Warrack attached a note disagreeing with some of the Report's conclusions, which was followed by a shorter note by Wakefield and Smith with some additional reservations. Laws did not sign and produced a separate report. PRO.HO.45/9648/A37324 contains correspondence regarding the duties of the Secretary.

### 56. Blind, Deaf and Dumb 1885-89

App. 28 July 1885. Rep. pres. 18 July 1889, C.5781-i, xix; C.5781-ii-iii, xx. Cost £7,562.

Duke of Westminster; Bishop of London; A.J. Mundella; F.J. Campbell; T.R. Armitage; W.T. Robertson.

Secretary: Charles Edward Drummond Black. (Named in Warr.)

Further Commissions of 13 Aug 1885 appointed Sir E.S. Sotheby and E.C. Johnson, and of 30 Oct 1885 W.A. Arrol and R. McDonnell.

**To investigate** and report on the condition of the blind in the United Kingdom and the various systems of education and employment available to them.

This was revoked by a Warrant of 20 Jan 1886 and a new Commission was appointed: Lord Egerton; Bishop of London; Sir L. Playfair; Mundella; Sir H.J. Selwin-Ibbetson; Sotheby; B. St. J. Ackers; Armitage; Arrol; Campbell; Johnson; McDonnell and Robertson. Black remained Secretary. The scope of the Commission was enlarged to include the Deaf and Dumb and others in need of exceptional methods of education.

A number of further Warrants were issued: 4 March 1886 appointing C. Few and W. Woodall; 27 Apr 1886, W.B. Sleight; 28 June 1886, C.M. Owen; 11 June 1887 L. Van Oven in place of Few who died 4 Apr 1887. McDonnell died 6 May 1889 and was not replaced.

All signed the final report with reservations by Ackers, Armitage, Campbell, Johnson, Sleight, Owen and Van Oven.

**57. Depression of Trade and Industry 1885-86**
App. 29 Aug 1885. Rep. (1) 7 Nov 1885: 1886, C.4621; (2) 31 March 1886, C.4715-i, xxi-ii; (3) 18 June 1886, C.4797; (4) 21 Dec 1886, C.4893, xxiii. Cost £1,612.
Earl of Iddesleigh; Earl of Dunraven & Mount-Earl; G. Sclater-Booth; Sir J.J. Allport; J. Aird; T. Birtwistle; L.L. Cohen; J.P. Corry; D. Dale; C.J. Drummond; W.F. Ecroyd; H.H. Gibbs; W.H. Houldsworth; W.L. Jackson; G.A. Jamieson; N. Lubbock; P.A. Muntz; A. O'Connor; R.H.I. Palgrave; C.M. Palmer; W. Pearce; B. Price; S. Storey.
Secretary: G.H. Murray. (Treasury; named in Warr.) Asst. Sec: T.H. Elliott.
**To inquire** and report upon the extent, nature, and probable causes of the depression now or recently prevailing in various branches of trade and industry, and whether it can be alleviated by legislative or other measures. (In full.)
It was originally proposed that the terms of reference be drawn up so as to enable the Commissioners to travel abroad thus avoiding the necessity of obtaining a separate sanction from the Treasury, but this course was resisted by both the Treasury and the Foreign Office and the Warrant did not contain the empowering clause. (PRO.HO.45/9656/A40724)
The Chairman circulated a memorandum for the Commission (P.P., 1885, (348), lxxi, 139) dated 12 Aug 1885 discussing the terms of reference, which are quoted in full above, and cautioning the Commission against too wide an inquiry. The proposed parameters for the inquiry are set out in two accompanying papers.
The first report consisted of the results of oral and written inquiries with no conclusions or recommendations. The third report was not signed by O'Connor, who added a dissent. The final report was signed with reservations by Sclater-Booth, Birtwistle, Cohen, Corry, Gibbs, Houldsworth, Jamieson, Palgrave, Palmer, Price and Storey. A minority report was signed by Ecroyd, Muntz, Lubbock and Dunraven, the latter subject to a reservation. Gibbs and Sclater-Booth also attached a note agreeing with some portions of this Report. O'Connor issued a separate minority report.

**58. Elementary Education Acts 1886-88**
App. 15 Jan 1886. Rep. (1) pres. 19 Aug 1886, C.4863, xxv; (2) 6 Apr 1887, C.5056, xxix; (3) 26 July 1887, C.5158, xxx; (4) 27 June (Majority) and 12 July (Dissenting), 1888, C.5485-i, xxxv; C.5485ii-iv, xxxvi; C.5329-i, xxxvii. Cost £6,357.
Sir R.A. Cross; Cardinal Archbishop Manning; Earl of Harrowby; Earl Beauchamp; Bishop of London; Lord Norton; A.J. Mundella; Sir F.R. Sandford; Sir J. Lubbock; Sir B. Samuelson; J.H. Rigg; R.W. Dale; R. Gregory; B.F. Smith; T.D.C. Morse; C.H. Alderson; J.G. Talbot; S.C. Buxton; T.E. Heller; B.C. Molloy; S. Rathbone; H. Richard; G. Shipton.
Secretary: H. Cowie, QC; d. c.1886, succ. by F.C. Bentinck. Asst. Sec: E.H.

Lyon.
The first Warrant was revoked and reissued on 10 March 1886, replacing
Mundella with the Hon. E.L. Stanley. A third Commission was issued on 15
June 1887 appointing the Duke of Norfolk in place of Molloy who had resigned.
**To enquire** into the working of the Elementary Education Acts, England and
Wales. (In full.)
The final majority report included reservations by Manning, Norton, Sandford,
Smith and Alderson. Stanley, Lubbock, Samuelson, Dale, Buxton, Heller,
Richard and Shipton issued a dissenting report, with a reservation by Buxton.
This was followed by a further report discussing the evidence taken by the
Commission and the general state of elementary education which was signed by
Stanley, Dale, Heller (with a reservation), Richard and Shipton.

## 59. Civil Establishments 1886-87
App. 20 Sept 1886. Rep. (1) 6 Sept 1887, C.5226, xix; (2) 10 Sept 1888,
C.5545, xxvii; (3) 5 June 1889 C.5748-i, xxi; (4) 30 July 1890, C.6172-i, xxvii.
Cost £2,220.
Sir M.W. Ridley; Earl Brownlow; Lord Rothschild; Lord Lingen; G.
Sclater-Booth (cr. Baron Basing, 1887); H.H. Fowler; Sir E.C. Guinness; A.B.
Freeman-Mitford; J. Cleghorn; A.S. Harvey; C.E. Lewis; A. O'Connor; P.
Rylands (d. 8 Feb 1887).
Secretary: H.G. Walpole. (Under Sec. of State to Principal Sec. of State for India;
named in Warr.)
A further Commission of 30 Nov 1887 appointed R.W. Hanbury, H.L.W. Lawson
and J.W. Maclure to replace Rylands; O'Connor, who according to the first report
'decline[d] his further co-operation ... for reasons entirely unconnected with the
Commission'; and Guinness who resigned.
This Commission was initiated by the Treasury and PRO.T.1/8248C gives details
of its appointment which was formalised by Memorandum, C.4883, and presented
to the House in Sept 1886. PRO.HO.45/9760/B661 is one of the most complete
of all the surviving Home Office files on Royal Commissions, with only one
piece missing (B.661.38). In addition to details about the submission of the
various reports it also contains documentation regarding the Commission's
inquiries into the Home Office itself, registering the reluctance of Home Office
staff to appear before the Commission, or even to make written submissions.
**To inquire** into the establishments of the different Offices of State at Home and
Abroad.
Lingen did not sign the first report and noted that although he agreed
substantially with its conclusions he felt that it should not have been presented
without further discussion. The second report was signed by all members, but
with dissenting notes from Rothschild, Lewis and Freeman Mitford. The third
report was signed with a note of disagreement by Lewis. Lawson did not sign

and attached his objections. The final report was signed subject to reservations by Hanbury, Lawson and Maclure. Lingen did not sign the main report, but signed under his note of reservation.

### 60. Relative Values of Gold and Silver 1886-88
App. 20 Sept 1886. Rep. (1) 10 June 1887, C.5099, xxii; (2) 30 Jan 1888, C.5248; (3) 31 Oct 1888, C.5512-i, xlv. Cost £1,652.
A.J. Balfour; J. Chamberlain; Hon. C.W. Fremantle; Sir J. Lubbock; Sir T.H. Farrer; J.R.B. Smith; D.M. Barbour; J.W. Birch; L.L. Cohen; L.H. Courtney; W.H. Houldsworth.
Secretary: G.H. Murray. (Named in Warr.)
Balfour became Chief Secretary for Ireland in 1887 and on 6 May 1887 the Warrant was revoked and reissued with Lord Herschell as Chairman, although Balfour remained on the Commission. With the exception of Bullen Smith the other members were reappointed and were joined by Sir L. Mallet and H. Chaplin. A further Warrant of 26 July 1887 appointed S. Montagu in the place of Cohen who had died. Chamberlain resigned in Sept 1887 and was not replaced.
To investigate the causes of recent changes in relative values of precious metals and especially to inquire whether these were due to (1) depreciation of silver; (2) depreciation of gold; (3) both. Further to inquire upon the bearing of these changes on practical business matters in India and the United Kingdom; if there had been serious effects to recommend ways of alleviating them. The Warrant is very detailed.
The final report has three parts, reflecting the divergent conclusions of the Commissioners: Part I was signed by all; Part II was signed by Herschell, Fremantle, Lubbock, Farrer, Birch and Courtney. Lubbock and Birch appended a note dissenting to some sections; Farrer attached a note clarifying one of the conclusions. Part III was signed by the remaining members, with a lengthy note by Mallet giving reasons for his adoption of Part III and for his dissent from Part II. Barbour wrote a similar note with 2 appendices, while Montagu attached a brief explanation of his views.

### 61. Mauritius 1886-87
App. 25 Sept 1886. Rep. 7 Jan 1887. Not presented to Parliament, but summarized in a Despatch written by H.T. Holland (Secretary of State for the Colonies), dated 12 July 1887, C.5101, lviii, 347. The costs were met from colonial funds.
Sir H.G.R. Robinson was appointed to inquire into the affairs of the Colony of Mauritius. (Taken from the *London Gazette*, 1 Oct 1886; the Warrant was not reprinted in full either in the *Gazette* or the Parliamentary Papers.)
Secretary: F.R. Round (Colonial Office); was appointed Colonial Secretary in

1887 and replaced by F.J. Newton, private secretary to Robinson. (PRO.T.1/1679) The enquiry was mainly concerned with charges of maladministration on the part of the governor, Sir J. Pope Hennessy. On the basis of the Commission's report Holland concluded that although mistakes had been made, there was not sufficient cause to justify his removal from office.

### 62. Warlike Stores 1886-88
App. 27 Sept 1886. Rep. (1) 16 May 1887, C.5062-i, xv; (2) 30 Apr 1888, C.5413, xxv, 541. Cost £995.
Sir J.F. Stephen; Sir A. Alison; Sir W.B. Barttelot; N. Salmon; J. Percy.
Secretary: J. Alleyne. (Army Colonel; named in Warr.)
**To inquire** into the system under which patterns of warlike stores were adopted and the stores obtained and passed for the service and whether any improvements could be made, also to investigate complaints or defects since 1 July 1881 to date of Warrant.
Salmon did not sign the final report.
A series of letters between Stephen and the Secretary of State for War, H.C.E. Childers, is included in the final report. Childers felt that the Commission had done him an injustice in stating that he took a decision on technical matters on which he was not qualified to judge. This interpretation was denied by Stephen, and as the matter was not resolved, the correspondence was printed in the Commission's papers.

### 63. Irish Land Laws 1886-87
App. 29 Sept 1886. Rep. 21 Feb 1887, C.4969-i-ii, C.5015 (separate report by Knipe), xxvi. Cost £2,953.
Earl Cowper; Earl of Milltown; Sir J. Caird; J.C. Neligan; G. Fottrell, Jnr.
Secretary: F.G. Hodder. (Barrister; named in Warr.)
**To inquire** and report to what extent the operation of the Land Law (Ireland) Act of 1881 was affected either by combinations to resist the enforcement of legal obligations or by an exceptional fall in the price of produce; and on the extent to which tenants had availed themselves of provisions of the Purchase of Land (Ireland) Act of 1885, and whether it might be improved or modified.
Fottrell resigned 1 Oct 1886 before the Commission had met and was replaced by Thomas Knipe.
Milltown attached a reservation to the report. Knipe did not sign and attached a letter explaining that he did not agree with many of the Commission's suggestions; and that as a tenant farmer he was unable and could not be expected to fully understand the meaning of the proposed legal changes. He issued a separate report dated 17 March 1887.

**64. Irish Public Works 1886-88**
App. 16 Oct 1886. Rep. (1) 9 Apr 1887, C.5038-i, xxv, 471; (2) 4 Jan 1888, C.5264-i, xlviii, 143. Cost £12,154.
Sir J.J. Allport; J. Abernethy; J.W. Barry; J.T. Pim.
Secretary: S.E.Spring-Rice. His appointment on 20 Oct 1886 was recorded in the *Dublin Gazette* of 22 Oct 1886, with that of W.F. Bailey, Assistant Secretary.
**To inquire** into the harbours, drainage and railways of Ireland, and the most appropriate means of financing their improvement.

**65. Market Rights 1887-91**
App. 5 July 1887. Rep. (1) 9 Aug 1888, C.5550, liii; (2) 15 Jan 1891: 1890-91, C.6268, xxxvii. Other papers: 1888, C.5550-i-iii, in liii-lv; 1889, C.5888-i, xxxviii; 1890-91, C.6268-i-vii in vols. xxxvii-xli inc. Cost £11,909.
Earl of Derby; Lord Balfour of Burleigh; H.C.E. Childers; Sir J.P. Corry; Sir T. Martineau; C.I. Elton; F.W. Maclean; H. Broadhurst; S. Charrington; J.J. Harwood; W.C. Little; J. McCarthy.
Secretary: T.B. Cockerton. (Barrister; named in Warr.)
Two further Warrants of 2 Jan 1888 and 18 Apr 1888 appointed J.A. Picton and P. Mahony respectively in place of Broadhurst and McCarthy, both of whom had resigned. Before the first report was signed Cockerton was replaced as Secretary by H.A.P. Rooke. Five Assistant Commissioners were appointed: B.F.C. Costelloe; A.J. Ashton; C.M. Chapman; C.W. Black; J.J. O'Meara.
**To inquire** into the holding of Market Rights and Tolls; how and under what authority they were exercised; and to report on any desirable legislative changes. The final report was signed by all the Commissioners but subject to reservations by Balfour, Childers, Corry, Martineau, Little, Picton and Mahony which they set out in a series of Supplementary Reports. Corry authorised the Secretary to sign for him as he had left England before the report was ready for signature.

**66. Malta 1887-88**
App. 17 Dec 1887. Rep. 7 Feb 1888, lxxiii, 634. Costs not included in the Parliamentary Returns for Royal Commissions. (RSM&S)
G.S. Baden-Powell and Sir G.F. Bowen.
Secretary: A. Froude.
**To inquire** into the manner of dividing the island of Malta and its dependencies into electoral districts.
Their report was not presented as a separate command paper but was contained within the Further Correspondence respecting the Constitution and Administration of Malta in the P.P. volume given above.

**67. Metropolitan Board of Works 1888-89**
App. 20 March 1888. Rep. (1) pres. 6 Nov 1888, C.5560, lvi; (2) 8 Apr 1889,

C.5705, xxxix, 319. Cost £927.
Lord Herschell; F.A. Bosanquet; H.R. Grenfell.
Secretary: V.A. Williamson. (Not named in either Warr. or report; HO file [below] records his appointment [24 March 1888] on Herschell's recommendation.)
**To inquire** into and report upon the working of the Metropolitan Board of Works, and into the irregularities which are alleged to have taken place in connection therewith. (In full.)
This Commission was given additional powers to compel the attendance of witnesses under the Metropolitan Board (Commission) Act 1888, 51 Vict. c.6. Following publication of the first report the Home Office sought an Opinion from the Treasury Solicitor as to whether proceedings should be brought against certain named officials of the Board who had already resigned their positions, but it was recommended (10 Nov 1888) that no further action should be taken. (PRO.HO.45/9776/B1926; B1926C)

### 68. University for London 1888-89
App. 2 May 1888. Rep. 29 Apr 1889, C.5709-i, xxxix, 323. Cost £907.
Earl of Selborne; J.T. Ball; Sir J. Hannen; Hon. G.C. Brodrick; Sir W. Thomson; G.G. Stokes; J.E.C. Welldon.
Secretary: J.L. Goddard. (Barrister; named in Warr.)
**To inquire** whether any and what kind of new university was required for the advancement of higher education in London.
The report was signed subject to reservations by Thomson, Stokes and Welldon. Brodrick had resigned before the report was completed.

### 69. Administration in the Army and Navy 1888-90
App. 7 June 1888. Rep. (1) 10 July 1889; (2) 11 Feb 1890, C.5979, xix. Cost £982.
Marquess of Hartington; Lord R.H. Spencer-Churchill; Lord Revelstoke; W.H. Smith; H. Campbell-Bannerman; Sir R. Temple; Sir F.W. Richards; H. Brackenbury; T.H. Ismay.
Joint Secretaries: G.S. Clarke and W.H. Hall.
**To inquire** into the civil and professional administration of the Naval and Military Departments, and their relation to each other and to the Treasury; and to report on what changes would lead to efficiency and economy in the Public Service.
All signed the first, preliminary, report subject to various dissensions and reservations from Churchill, Temple, Richards, Brackenbury and Ismay. The final report was signed by all with reservations from Campbell-Bannerman, Temple, Brackenbury and Ismay.
PRO.HO.45/9791/B4267 gives details of the disposal of the Commission's

papers; some papers were sent to the Record Office, where their receipt was acknowledged on 17 Nov 1892. Those papers which were judged to be less important were sent to the Stationery Office to be confidentially destroyed. (File note of 14 Nov 1892.)

### 70. Welsh Sunday Closing 1889-90
App. 25 May 1889. Rep. pres. 31 March 1890, C.5994-i; C.5994A, Welsh translation, xl. Cost £2,035.
Lord Balfour of Burleigh; Viscount Emlyn; J.T. Hibbert; Sir R. Harington; H. Lloyd.
Secretary: J. Rhys (Jesus Professor of Celtic at University of Oxford; named in Warr.), who also acted as interpreter since a number of witnesses spoke only Welsh.
**To inquire** into the operation of the Sunday Closing (Wales) Act 1881.
PRO.HO.45/9806/B6168A contains correspondence between the Home Office and Treasury about the Welsh translation of the report which it was agreed should be undertaken by Professor Rhys for a fee of no more than £50. The completed translation was received by the Home Office on 28 May 1890, but it was recommended that it should not be laid before Parliament as it would be unintelligible to most of the members.

### 71. Vaccination 1889-97
App. 29 May 1889. Rep. (1) 12 Aug 1889, C.5845, xxxix, 657; (2) 29 May 1890, C.6066; (3) 7 Aug 1890, C.6192, xxxix, 367; (4) 28 July 1891: 1890-91, C.6527, xliv, 735; (5) 21 Apr 1892, C.6666, xlvii, 547; (6) 14 Feb 1896, C.7993, xlvii; (7) pres. 14 Aug 1896, C.8270, xlvii, 889. Appendices: 1897, C.8609-15, xlv-xlvii. Cost £13,040.
Lord Herschell; Sir J. Paget; Sir C. Dalrymple; Sir W.G. Hunter; Sir E.H. Galsworthy; W.S. Savory (d. 4 March 1895); C. Bradlaugh; J.S. Bristowe (d. 20 Aug 1895); W.J. Collins; J.S. Dugdale; M. Foster; J. Hutchinson; J.A. Picton; S. Whitbread; F.M. White.
Secretary: B. Ince.
A second Commission of 8 Apr 1891 appointed J.A. Bright to replace Bradlaugh who had died 30 Jan 1891.
**To inquire** and report as to the effects of vaccination in reducing death from smallpox; alternatives to vaccination for reducing the disease; and alterations in the provisions under the Vaccination Acts.
Collins and Picton did not sign the final report, appending a lengthy statement of the grounds for their dissent; they also signed a note of dissension with Whitbread and Bright (who had both signed the report). Hunter and Hutchinson signed subject to a note of dissent.
PRO.HO.45/9810/B6619 contains documentation of a number of cases where

legal action was taken against persons who failed to comply with the Vaccination Acts, as well as correspondence relating to the premature publication of the report. It was decided to amend the instructions to Secretaries so as to stress their responsibility for keeping the contents of the report confidential until it had been sent to the Queen and presented to Parliament.

Collins wrote a memoir of his work on the Commission, possibly intended for publication, which is held with his papers at the University of London Library. (MS.812/164)

## 72. Mining Royalties 1889-93

App. 14 Aug 1889. Rep. (1) 31 July 1890, C.6195, xxxvi; (2) 31 March 1891, (3) 22 July 1891: 1890-91, C.6331, and C.6529, xli, 375, & 817; (4) 8 March 1893, C.6979; (5) 24 March 1893: 1893-4, C.6980, xli. Cost £6,012.

Earl of Northbrook; Lord Macnaghten; Sir W.T. Lewis; W. Abraham; A. Barnes; T. Burt; D. Dale; G.B. Forster; H.H. Gibbs; A. Hood; G.A. Jamieson; W. Kenrick; J. Knowles; J.E.C. Munro; W.C. Pendarves; C.T. Redington; F.P. Rhodes; R.C. Robertson; J. Thomas; C.A. Whitmore; N. Wood (d. 1893). Secretary: H. Lyon.

To inquire into royalties paid on metals of United Kingdom mines subject to the Metalliferous Mines Act of 1872 and into the terms and conditions under which mining enterprise was conducted in India, the Colonies and Foreign Countries.

## 73. Westminster Abbey 1890-91

App. 26 Apr 1890. Rep. (1) 30 July 1890, C.6228; (2) 24 June 1891: 1890-91, C.6398, xliv, 575. Cost £988.

D.R. Plunket; Sir A.H. Layard; Sir F. Leighton; G.G. Bradley; L.J. Jennings; A. Waterhouse. Secretary: Hon. H. Dillon.

To inquire into the present state of the Abbey of Westminster as regards space for interment and memorials.

The final report was signed by all, but with a note of dissension to the last paragraph from Layard, Leighton and Bradley.

## 74. Tuberculosis 1890-95

App. 21 July 1890. Rep. 3 Apr 1895, C.7703, xxxv, 615. Other papers: 1896, C.7992, xlvi. Cost £6,156.

Lord Basing; G.T. Brown; G. Buchanan (ktd. 1892); J.F. Payne; J.B. Sanderson. Secretary: C.E.L.B. Hudson. (Physician; named in Warr.)

Basing died 22 Oct 1894 and a new Commission was warranted on 15 Nov 1894, with Buchanan as Chairman, but there were no other new appointments.

To inquire and report on the effect of food from tuberculous animals on human health.

The report was signed by all members; Brown produced a further report 10 Apr 1895.

### 75. Redemption of Tithe in England and Wales 1891-92
App. 31 Jan 1891. Rep. 18 Feb 1892, C.6606-i, xlvii, 341. Cost £636.
Lord Basing; G. Cubitt; H.H. Fowler; Sir H.H. Vivian; F.M. White; W.J. Beadel; C.N. Dalton.
Secretary: J. Graham. (Bd. of Agriculture; named in Warr.)
**To inquire** into the redemption of tithe rentcharge in England and Wales under the Tithe Commutation Act 1836 and its amendments, and to report on any changes which might be required.
PRO.HO.45/9834/B10005 concerns the non-payment of the Secretary. The Treasury view, which prevailed, was that as Graham was already in receipt of a salary from the Board of Agriculture he was not entitled to the payment of £400 per annum which was usual for Secretaries of Royal Commissions, but they were prepared to authorise a gratuity of £250 (25 Aug 1892).

### 76. Explosions in Mines 1890-94
App. 9 Feb 1891. Rep. (1) 30 July 1891: 1890-91, C.6543, xxii, 555; (2) 13 June 1894, C.7401-i, xxiv, 583. Cost £1,783.
J. Chamberlain; Lord Rayleigh; Sir W.T. Lewis; H.B. Dixon; E. Bainbridge; C. Fenwick.
Secretary: J. Wilson.
**To inquire** into the effect of coal dust in the cause of explosions in mines and whether there were any practicable means to prevent or mitigate any dangers caused by coal dust.

### 77. Labour 1891-94
App. 21 Apr 1891. Rep. (1) 16 March 1892, C.6708, xxxiv; (2) 20 June 1892, C.6795, xxxvi, Pt.1; (3) 2 Feb 1893: 1893-4, C.6894, xxxii; (4) 1 June 1893: 1893-4, C.7063, xxxix, pt.1; (5) 24 May 1894, C.7421, xxxv, 9; Secretary's Report C.7421-i, 263. Other papers: 1892, C.6708-i-vi, xxxiv & xxxv; C.6795-i-xii, xxxvi, Pt.2-5; 1893-4, C.6894-i-xxv, xxxii-xxxvii; C.7063-iv-vC, xxxviii; C.7063-i-iiiA, xxxix, pt.1; C.7063-vi-xiv, xxxix, pt.2; 1894, C.7540, xxxv. Cost £31,235*.
Marquess of Hartington (Duke of Devonshire, Dec 1891); Earl of Derby (d. 21 Apr 1893); Sir M.E. Hicks-Beach; A.J. Mundella; H.H. Fowler; L.H. Courtney; Sir J.E. Gorst; Sir F. Pollock; Sir E.J. Harland; Sir W.T. Lewis; A. Marshall; W. Abraham; M. Austin; G.W. Balfour; J.C. Bolton; T. Burt; J. Collings; D. Dale; A. Hewlett; T.H. Ismay; G. Livesey; T. Mann; J. Mawdsley; S. Plimsoll; H. Tait; E. Trow; W. Tunstill.
Joint Secretaries: G. Drage and J. Burnett. Asst. Sec: F.V. Hornby.

Senior Asst. Commissioner: W.C. Little. Senior Lady Asst. Commissioner: Miss E. Orme. Asst. Commissioners: Miss M. Abraham; W.E. Bear; C.M. Chapman; Miss C.E. Collet; A.W. Fox; G.R. Gillespie (d. 13 Oct 1892); Miss M.H. Irwin; R. McCrea; W.P. O'Brien; R.H. Pringle; R.C. Richards; H. Rutherford; A.J. Spencer; D.L. Thomas; E. Wilkinson.

The four women named above were the first women appointed to be Assistant Commissioners. The Secretary's report also notes the appointment of women to both skilled and routine positions on the staff of the Commission, and records how successfully they had carried out their work. The total number of clerks on the Commission was twenty-seven, of whom twenty-one were women; thirteen of these were Oxbridge graduates. However Drage's public celebration of his female staff needs to be qualified by the lengthy statement of one clerk, Miss Wilson, of her claim against wrongful dismissal (PRO.HO.45/9837/B10296/102).

**To inquire** into the relations between employer and employed; combinations of employers and employed; conditions of labour, which had been raised during the recent trade disputes in the United Kingdom; and to report on whether and what legislation would help to remedy any evils that may be disclosed.

The Commission formed three sub-committees to cope with its wide-reaching terms of reference, these were chaired by Dale, Derby and Mundella. The final report was split: eighteen of the Commissioners signed the majority report; Lewis, Bolton, Livesey, Devonshire, Dale, Hicks-Beach, Courtney, Pollock, Ismay, Tunstill, Collings and Trow appended various observations and minor dissensions. Two minority reports were produced: the first by Abraham, Austin, Mawdsley and Mann; the second by Gorst. Fowler and Tait did not sign.

At the end of the Commission Drage published a book entitled *The Unemployed* (Macmillan 1894), which was highly critical of the Board of Trade. Courtenay Boyle (Permanent Secretary, Bd. of Trade) wrote to the Home Department (24 July 1894) to record that it was 'entirely opposed to the interests of the Public Service that Secretaries of Royal Commissions should be allowed to publish documents assailing Departments of State' and 'if the precedent created by it were followed in other cases, would tend greatly to impair those Inter-Departmental courtesies and amenities upon which the administration of the affairs of the State so largely depends'. Home Office advice was that no action could be taken although such impropriety meant that Drage would no longer be considered for public office. (PRO.HO.45/9837/B10296A) However this prohibition was not permanent and in October 1917 he took up the appointment of Director of Investigations for the Board of Agriculture. See also PRO.HO.45/9842/B11168; 9837/B10296. He also wrote a number of other publications which drew upon the work of the Commission, including *The Problem of the Aged Poor* (1895), and *The Labour Problem* (1896).

*This was not the total cost which was estimated at £50,000.

### 78. Metropolitan Water Supply 1892-93
App. 15 March 1892. Rep. 8 Sept 1893: 1893-4, C.7172-i, xl, Pt.1. Other papers: C.7172-ii-iv, xl, Pt.2. Cost £4,720.
Lord Balfour of Burleigh; Sir G.B. Bruce; Sir A. Geikie; J. Dewar; G.H. Hill; J. Mansergh; W. Ogle.
Secretary: F. Gaskell.
**To inquire** into the adequacy of quantity and quality of the metropolitan water supply.
PRO.HO.45/9864/B13728: Files relating to petitions and correspondence, 1890-98.

### 79. Draft Charter for proposed Gresham University in London 1892-94
App. 30 Apr 1892. Rep. 24 Jan 1894: 1893-4, C.7259, xxxi, 807. Other papers: 1894, C.7425-i, xxxiv. Cost £2,823.
Earl Cowper; Lord Reay; Bishop Barry; Sir L. Playfair; Sir W.S. Savory; Sir G.M. Humphry; G.G. Ramsay; G.F. Browne; H. Sidgwick; J.S.B. Sanderson; J. Anstie; R.C. Palmer; G.H. Rendall.
Secretary: J.L. Goddard. (Barrister; named in Warr.)
**To consider** and, if necessary, amend, alter or extend the proposed Charter for the Gresham University in London.
Bishop Barry, Savory, Humphry, Palmer, Rendall, Browne, Reay, Sidgwick and Anstie attached dissenting notes and alternative recommendations. The Commission recommended that the University should apply for a new charter to enable it to become a teaching University and that if such an application was received by Her Majesty they would then make a further report. This raised a dilemma for the Home Office which had to decide whether or not the Commission could prolong its existence in this way, but after some deliberation it was decided that with the production of a report and its presentation to the Queen, a Commission was deemed to have ceased. (PRO.HO.45/9774/B1659)

### 80. Lighthouses 1892-98
App. 13 June 1892. Rep. (1) 8 Dec 1892: 1893-4, C.6844, xxxi; (2) pres. 9 Apr 1894, C.7338, xxxiii, 367; (3) 26 Apr 1895, C.7736, xxxv, 351; (4) 12 May 1896, C.8092, xxxiii, 35; (5) pres. 8 Feb 1898, C.8675, xxxiii, 213. Cost £3,059.
Earl of Mount-Edgcumbe; Sir E. Birkbeck; Sir F.L. M'Clintock; Sir G.S. Nares; J.C. Lamb; R.C. Munro-Ferguson; E. Graves; J.A. Kempe; H.L. Mulholland.
Secretary: G. Roper. (Named in Warr.)
Subsequent Commissions of 26 Nov 1892, and 21 June 1893 appointed W.H. Preece in place of Graves who died 9 Nov 1892; and E.G. Moggridge as Secretary in place of Roper who had resigned.
**To inquire** and report what lighthouses and light-vessels should be connected to the telegraphic system of the United Kingdom ... without impairing the efficiency

of the Light Service.

## 81. Highlands and Islands 1892-95
App. 6 Dec 1892. Rep. 19 March 1895, C.7681, xxxviii. Other papers: C.7668, xxxviii & C.7668i-ii, xxxix pts. 1&2. Cost £11,365. (LPGS)
D. Brand; M.H. Shaw-Stewart; A. Sutherland; J.N.M. Forsyth; G. Gordon; J.M. M'Callum; J. Macleod; H. Munro.
Secretary: W. Mackenzie.
**To inquire** into whether land in the counties of Argyll, Inverness, Ross and Cromarty, Sutherland, Caithness, and Orkney and Shetland currently used for deer forests, grouse moors or other sporting purposes could be used for cultivation by crofters or other small tenants.
Forsyth authorised the chairman to sign for him as he had left the country before the report was prepared. Shaw-Stewart, Forsyth, Gordon, MacCallum and Munro added various reservations.

## 82. Aged Poor 1893-95
App. 7 Jan 1893. Rep. 26 Feb 1895, C.7684-i, xiv; C.7684-ii, xv. Cost £2,364.
Lord Aberdare; Prince of Wales; Lord Lingen; Lord Brassey; Lord Playfair; J. Chamberlain; C.T. Ritchie; Sir H.E. Maxwell; J.J. Henley; A. Pell; W.A. Hunter; J. Stuart; A.C. Humphreys-Owen; C.S. Roundell; C.S. Loch; J. Arch; C. Booth; H. Broadhurst; J.J. Stockall.
Secretary: E.A. Browne. (Barrister; named in Warr.) Asst. Sec: Viscount Morpeth. Browne was awarded a gratuity of £600, more than twice the usual amount, in recognition of the importance and difficulty of his work. (PRO.T.13/23/507 and 560)
**To consider** whether any alterations in the system of Poor Law Relief are desirable, in the case of persons whose destitution is occasioned by incapacity for work, resulting from old age, or whether assistance could otherwise be afforded in those cases. (In full.)
Lord Aberdare died on 25 Feb 1895, the day before the report was ready for signature; he had been ill for some time and had been replaced as Chairman by Playfair who had been unanimously elected by his colleagues on 11 Dec 1894. Hunter was also unable to sign the report due to illness.
The Prince of Wales did not sign the report as he feared to compromise his political neutrality since the subject of the Commission had become one of party controversy. The majority report was signed by Lingen, Brassey, Playfair, Henley, Pell, Humphreys-Owen, Roundell, Loch, Arch and Stockall - all subject to appended memoranda. Stuart wrote a minority report and also signed a memorandum with Brassey, Humphreys-Owen and Arch qualifying their support for the views of the majority. Two other minority reports were produced: the first by Chamberlain, Ritchie, Maxwell, Hunter and Booth, with additional

memoranda from Ritchie and Booth; and the second by Broadhurst.

### 83. Welsh Land 1893-96
App. 27 March 1893. Rep. (1) 29 June 1894, C.7439, xxxvi; (2) 26 Aug 1896, C.8221, xxxiv. Other papers: 1894, C.7439-i-ii, xxxvi, xxxvii; 1895, C.7661, xl; C.7757, xli; 1896, C.8242, xxxiii, 555; C.8222, xxxv. Cost £8,432.
Lord Carrington; Lord Kenyon; Sir J.T.D. Llewelyn; D.B. Jones; J. Rhys; J.M. Griffiths; E. Grove; R. Jones; F. Seebohm.
Secretary: D.L. Thomas. Asst. Sec: C.E. Owen. Thomas was unable to work for several months because of illness and Owen became co-secretary on 6 March 1895. (PRO.T.13/23/482 and HO.45 ref. below)
**To inquire** into the conditions and circumstances under which land in Wales and Monmouthshire is held, occupied and cultivated, and to report thereupon. (In full.)
A minority report was signed by Kenyon, Llewelyn and Seebohm.
There were several cases of alleged intimidation of witnesses to the Commission. Legal opinion was sought as to whether these could be prosecuted under the terms of the Witnesses Protection Act of 1892, but no action was taken.
The Commissioners wanted to have part of their report translated into Welsh and the files record the prolonged correspondence regarding this, which includes a list of those official papers translated into Welsh - a practice apparently only begun by the Home Office with the Metalliferous Mines Act of 1873. The practice of other government departments in this matter was given in another Home Office file, their ref. A.47143B. (PRO.HO.45/9869/B14051)

### 84. Unification of London 1893-94
App. 27 March 1893. Rep. 7 Aug 1894, C.7493-i, xvii; C.7493-ii, xviii. Cost £1,299.
L.H. Courtney; Sir T.H. Farrer; R.D. Holt; H.H. Crawford; E.O. Smith.
Secretary: G.E.Y. Gleadowe (app. by a separate Warr. of 5 Apr 1893).
**To consider** the proper conditions under which the amalgamation of the City and the County of London can be effected, and to make specific and practical proposals for that purpose. (In full.)
Crawford did not sign the report.

### 85. Opium 1893-95
App. 2 Sept 1893. Rep. (1) 30 Dec 1893: 1894, C.7313, lx, 583; (2) 16 Apr 1895, C.7723-i, xlii, 31. Other papers: 1894, C.7397, C.7419, lxi; C.7471, C.7473, lxii; 1895, C.7751, xlii. Cost £18,503.
Lord Brassey; Sir J.B. Lyall; Maharajah of Darbhanga; Sir W. Roberts; R.G.C. Mowbray; A.U. Fanshawe; A. Pease; H. Viharidas; H.J. Wilson.
Secretary: J.P. Hewett (Dept. Sec. to Govt. of India in Home Dept; named in

Warr.); took up an appointment in India and was succeeded by J.A. Baines, appointed by Warrant of 28 May 1894.

**To report** on the effects of prohibition of the growth and sale of opium, except for medical purposes, in British India and whether this could be extended to the Native States.

The final report was signed subject to a qualifying memorandum by Singh and Veharidas. Wilson did not sign and wrote a Minute of Dissent, 18 March 1895, printed as Appendix IV of the report. C.7751 is a supplement to the report by the Maharajah of Darbhanga.

## 86. Agricultural Depression 1893-97

App. 14 Sept 1893. Rep. (1) 4 May 1894, C.7400, xvi, Pt.1. (2) 7 Feb 1896, C.7981, xvi, 413; (3) 25 June 1897, C.8540, xv. Other papers: 1894, C.7400-i, C.7365, C.7372, C.7334, C.7374, C.7342, xvi, Pt.1; C.7400-ii-iii, xvi Pt.2 & Pt.3. 1895, C.7728, C.7691, C.7671, C.7755, C.7623, C.7624, C.7735, xvi; C.7842, C.7871, C.7764, C.7915-i, C.7625, C.7742, xvii. 1896, C.8125, xvi, 469; C.8021 and C.8146, xvii. 1897, C.8541 and C.8300, xv. Cost £12,206.

G.J. Shaw-Lefevre; Viscount Cobham; Lord Vernon; H. Chaplin; Sir R.N.F. Kingscote; R. Giffen; C.I. Elton; O. Thomas; F.A. Channing; J. Clay; C.N. Dalton; R.L. Everett; J. Gilmour; G. Lambert; W.C. Little; W.H. Long; C. Whitehead.

Secretary: H. Lyon. (Named in Warr.) Asst. Sec: R.F. Crawford.

A Commission of 3 May 1894 appointed Lord Rendel in place of Vernon who resigned. Shaw-Lefevre resigned as Chairman on 20 Apr 1896 and on 19 May Lyon informed the Home Office that the Commissioners had elected Cobham to replace him. Lyon had previously (8 May) requested guidance from the Home Office on Shaw-Lefevre's position. He had resigned as Chairman because of his deep disagreement with his colleagues, but wanted to remain a member so that he could make his report. However the Home Office advised Lyon that to resign as Chairman implied resignation from the Commission. (PRO.HO.45/9875/B15063)

The Commission appointed eight Assistant Commissioners: W. Fream; J. Turner; A.W. Fox; R.H. Pringle; J. Hope; R.H. Rew; A. Spencer; J. Speir. The file (ref. above) records Treasury disquiet at the number of Assistant Commissioners and the length of time for which they were employed. One of the Commissioners, Mr Clay, a tenant farmer, was paid for his attendance at meetings at the rate of two guineas a day to compensate him for loss of earnings.

**To inquire** into the Agricultural Depression prevailing in Great Britain, and whether it could be alleviated by legislation or other measures.

The dissent which was so marked in the affairs of this Commission surfaced over the publication of its second report, which was signed by the majority with reservations and memoranda from Cobham, Thomas, Clay and Everett. All the signatories produced a series of supplementary reports which were followed by an objection to the majority's reports by Shaw-Lefevre, Rendel, Giffen and Lambert who considered it exceptional if not unprecedented for a Commission to present as an interim report one which recorded so much disagreement between members. Shaw-Lefevere, Rendel and Giffen produced a minority report with further, separate reports by Channing and Lambert.

The final report was signed by fourteen Commissioners, ten of whom wrote a supplementary report. They all signed one or more of the nine reservations or memoranda which followed the reports. Lambert and Channing again produced separate minority reports.

The troubles of the Commission continued after their report was published: when Lyon asked for guidance from the Home Office on the disposal of the Commission's documents (16 July 1897), the file cover emphatically stated that 'The Board of Agriculture will have nothing to do with them'. It was left to him to decide which of the documents were to be destroyed and which to be sent to the Record Office, the Home Office insisting that this was not their responsibility.

### 87. Dominica 1893-94
App. 22 Sept 1893. Rep. 10 March 1894, C.7477, lvii, 145. Costs met from Colonial Funds. (RSM&S)
Sir Robert George Crookshank Hamilton was appointed **to inquire** into causes of discontent, and the working of the political constitution of Dominica.
Secretary: R.W. Hamilton. (Son of the above.)

### 88. Secondary Education in England 1894-96
App. 2 March 1894. Rep. 13 Aug 1895, C.7862 xliii. Other papers: 1895, C.7862-i-viii, xliv-xlix; 1896, C.8077, xlvi. Cost £5,329.
J. Bryce; Sir J.T. Hibbert; Hon. E. Lyttelton; Sir H.E. Roscoe; E.C. Maclure; A.M. Fairbairn; R.C. Jebb; R. Wormell; H. Hobhouse; M.E. Sadler; H.L. Smith; G.J. Cockburn; C. Fenwick; J.H. Yoxall; Lady F. Cavendish; Mrs S. Bryant; Mrs E.M. Sidgwick.
Secretary: Hon. W.N. Bruce. (Barrister; named in Warr.)
**To consider** what are the best methods of establishing a well-organised system of secondary education in England, taking into account existing deficiencies and having regard to such local sources of revenue from endowment or otherwise as are available or may be made available for this purpose, and to make recommendations accordingly. (In full.)
This Commission was the first to include women as full Commissioners. The Commission appointed fourteen Assistant Commissioners: R.E. Mitcheson; H.T. Gerrans; Mrs E.S. Armitage; F.E. and Mrs F.A. Kitchener; A.J. Butler; W. and Mrs E.P. Lee Warner; J. Headlam; J. Massie; Mrs G. Jones; A.P. Laurie; Miss

C.L. Kennedy; J.J. Findlay, whose reports are in C.7862-v-vi. The Treasury authorised payment for only four - Gerrans, Kitchener, Butler and Laurie - at a rate of £10 a week for a period not exceeding four months. The appointment of an Assistant Secretary was refused but a sum of £7.10s. per week was granted to cover all clerical assistance on condition that no one was to receive more than £3 a week and that no copyist was to get more than 30s. a week. (PRO.HO.45/9880/B15884)

## 89. Financial Relations between Great Britain and Ireland 1894-96
App. 26 May 1894. Rep. (1) 28 March 1895, C.7720-i, xxxvi; (2) pres. 13 Aug 1896, C.8262 xxxiii, 59. Other papers, C.7720-ii, same vol. Cost £1,968.
H.C.E. Childers; Lord Farrer; Lord Welby; C.O. O'Conor; Sir R.G.C. Hamilton (d. 22 Apr 1895); Sir T. Sutherland; Sir D.M. Barbour; Hon. E. Blake; B.W. Currie; W.A. Hunter; C.E. Martin; J.E. Redmond; T. Sexton.
Secretary: B.H. Holland. (Barrister; named in Warr.)
A Warrant of 22 June 1894 appointed H.F. Slattery and G.W. Wolff to the Commission.
Childers died 29 Jan 1896 and Holland wrote to the Home Office 30 Jan (PRO:HO45/9882/B16301) requesting advice on the procedure for appointing a new Chairman. A letter of 11 Feb notes that Lord Farrer, the second named person on the Warrant, was in Egypt and not expected to return until the end of March. Holland was advised that the Secretary of State thought it inadvisable for an outside appointment to be made at such a late stage of the Commission's proceedings and that the best course would be for them to select one of their members. The file note cites as precedent the Commission on the Aged Poor (no. **82**); O'Conor was subsequently chosen as Chairman.
**To inquire** into the financial relations between Great Britain and Ireland and their relative taxable capacity and to report how the latter might be most equitably determined.
The final majority report was signed subject to a series of reservations and memoranda; Barbour and Sutherland produced separate minority reports. The papers also include Childers's draft report.

## 90. Tweed and Solway Fisheries 1895-96
App. 1 May 1895. Rep. (1) Solway, pres. 6 Aug 1896, C.8182-3, xlvi, 503; (2) Tweed, pres. 13 May 1896, C.8086-7, xlvi, 731. Cost £1,182.
E.S. Howard; R. Neville; A.D. Berrington; R.W. Cochran-Patrick; J. Cheyne; J.J. Armistead.
Secretary: T.A.C. Hampson. (Barrister; named in Warr.)
A subsequent Warrant of 9 Sept 1895 appointed J.W. Mellor to replace Neville who had resigned.
**To inquire** into and report upon the salmon and freshwater fisheries of the

Tweed river and the Solway Firth.

**91. Military and Civil Expenditure in India 1895-1900**
App. 24 May 1895. Rep. (1) 10 Aug 1896, C.8258, xv; (2) 6 Apr 1900, Cd.131, xxix, 553. Other papers: 1896, C.8259, xvi; 1900, Cd.130, xxix; Paper no. 387, Sess. 2, lvii, 431; 1902, Paper no. 169, lxx, 515. Cost £4,242 - half of which was charged to Indian Revenues.
Lord Welby; L.H. Courtney; W.L. Jackson; Hon. G.N. Curzon; Sir W. Wedderburn; Sir D.M. Stewart (d. 26 March 1900); Sir E.W. Hamilton; Sir J.B. Peile; Sir A.R. Scoble; R.H. Knox (ktd. 1895); G.L. Ryder; T.R. Buchanan; W.S. Caine; D. Naoroji.
Secretary: R.T.W. Ritchie. (Named in Warr.) He resigned and was replaced by C.G. Campbell, appointed by a Warrant of 9 Aug 1895; the file notes that a shortened form of Warrant was used for the first time. Campbell had been private secretary to the Secretary of State for India 1894-5, and Ritchie succeeded him in this post where he remained until 1902. Ritchie continued to be involved in the affairs of the Commission; the later correspondence from the Home Office about the publication of the second report was addressed to him. (See below)
Curzon resigned upon his appointment as Under Secretary of State to the Principal Secretary for Foreign Affairs and a Warrant 3 Feb 1896 appointed R.G.C. Mowbray in his place.
**To inquire** into the administration and management of the Military and Civil expenditure incurred under the authority of the Secretary of State for India in Council, or of the Government of India, and the apportionment of charge between the Governments of the United Kingdom and India for purposes in which both are interested. (In full.)
A question was put down in Parliament (16 May 1899) about the Commission's failure to report. According to Home Office records the last meeting had been held on 27 July 1897 and since no report had been produced the Commission was technically in breach of its Warrant. Ritchie was advised that the Secretary did not have power to summon members but could arrange for a meeting to be held and if there was a quorum (in this case, five) they could proceed in execution of the Commission. As an extreme step there was no doubt that the Secretary could advise the Crown to dissolve the Commission if they refused to meet and execute their Commission, although there was no recent precedent for this. There was a record of one case in 1854 in which Lord Palmerston threatened a Commission (not named) that if they did not report before a certain date he would recommend that their allowances and expenses should not be paid. This was not seen as an appropriate sanction in the present case, however, as the Commission no longer appeared in the estimates. There had been many cases in which the Home Office had had to make 'strong representations to Chairmen of Commissions with respect to the conduct of the Commission or delay in issuing

or other matters connected with the Report; but these matters, so far as our records show, are dealt with semi-officially and generally through the Secretary of the Commission' (Home Office to Ritchie 16 May 1899.) (PRO.HO. 45/9898/B18480)

The final report was signed subject to reservations by Welby, Knox, Peile, Scoble, Ryder, Buchanan and Mowbray. Wedderburn and Naoroji produced a minority report which was signed, with reservations, by Caine.

## 92. Laws on Intoxicating Liquor 1896-99

App. 24 Apr 1896. Rep. (1) pres. 24 Feb 1897, C.8355-6, xxxiv, 247; (2) pres. 25 June 1897, C.8523-i, xxxv; (3) pres. 8 Feb 1898, C.8693, xxxvi; (4) pres. 18 Apr 1898, C.8821-2, xxxviii; (5) pres. 3 Aug 1898, C.8979, xxxviii; (6) 22 June 1899, C.9379, xxxiv. Other papers: 1898, C.8694, xxxvi; C.8695-6, xxxvii; C.8980, xxxviii; 1899, C.9075, xxxiv, 441; C.9076, C9379-i, xxxv. Cost £8,080. Viscount Peel; Earl of Jersey; Viscount de Vesci; Bishop of London (became Archbishop of Canterbury in 1897); Sir A.E. West; Sir W.H. Houldsworth; Sir F.S. Hunt; Sir C. Cameron; H.H. Dickinson; W. Allen; W.S. Caine; A.M. Gordon; W. Graham; H. Grinling; S. Hyslop; A. Johnston; J.H. Roberts; H.R. Smith; C. Walker; J.L. Wharton; T.P. Whittaker; A.M. Wigram; S. Young; G. Younger.

Secretary: S. Peel. Asst. Sec: H. Delacombe.

Warrants of 7 May 1897 and 16 Apr 1898 respectively appointed Lord Windsor and E.N. Buxton to replace the Earl of Jersey and Hunt who had resigned.

**To inquire** into the operation and administration of laws relating to the sale of intoxicating liquors and to report on proposals to change the laws, having regard to the rights of individuals.

Twenty-one of the twenty-four commissioners signed the first report; the following four were signed by all without dissent. Vesci*, Windsor, West, Dickinson*, Allen*, Buxton, Gordon, Graham, Grinling*, Hyslop*, Johnston, Riley Smith*, Walker*, Wharton, Wigram*, Young* and Younger* signed the final majority report.

*Subject to various reservations appended.

The minority report was signed by the Chairman, Archbishop of Canterbury*, Houldsworth?, Cameron*, Dickinson?, Allen?, Caine*, Roberts* and Whittaker*, some of whom also signed the majority report.

* With addenda.
? Subject to reservations.

PRO.HO.45/10151/B.20998 has several files relating to the legislation to be adopted as a result of the Commission's recommendations. It also contains correspondence regarding the publication of minority reports. The Secretary had asked if the Chairman's minority report should take precedence over the majority report in the printed Command paper, but the Home Office replied that a search had been made for a period of twelve years and no record could be found for a minority report being printed first. Under the terms of the Commission 'the Report which is signed by a majority of the members is, strictly speaking, the expression of the opinion of the Commission, and should appear first in the Report submitted to Her Majesty'. (Home Office to Secretary Peel, 2 June 1899)

## 93. Control of trade from tuberculous animals 1896-98
App. 6 July 1896. Rep. 4 Apr 1898, C.8824, xlix, 333; Evidence, C.8831. Cost £2,081.
Sir H.E. Maxwell; R.T. Thorne; G.T. Brown; H.E. Clare; S.F. Murphy; J. Speir; T. Cooke-Trench.
Secretary: T.M. Legge. (Named in Warr.)
**To inquire** and report what administrative procedures were available for controlling danger to man from the use of meat and milk of tuberculous animals. Maxwell, Clare and Cooke-Trench attached a Memorandum to the report.

## 94. Local Taxation 1896-1902
App. 15 Aug 1896. Rep. (1) 16 Dec 1898: 1899, C.9141, xxxv, 733; (2) 10 Jan 1899, C.9142, xxxv, 795; (3) 28 May 1901, Cd.638, xxiv, 413; (4) 14 Feb 1902, Cd. 973; 10 Apr 1902, Cd.1067; 11 Apr 1902, Cd.1068, xxxix. Other papers: 1898, C.8763, xli; C.8764-5, xlii; 1899, C.9150, C.9319, C.9528, xxxvi; 1900, Cd.201, Cd.383, xxxvi; 1902, Cd.1221, xxxix; 1903, Cd.1480, xxiii. Cost £7,234.
Lord Balfour of Burleigh; Viscount Emlyn (became Earl Cawdor in March 1898); J.B. Balfour; Sir J.T. Hibbert; C.B. Stuart-Wortley; Sir E.W. Hamilton; Sir A. Milner; C.N. Dalton; C.A. Cripps; H.E. Clare; T.H. Elliott; A. O'Connor; E.O. Smith; J. Stuart; J.L. Wharton.
Secretary: A.W. Fox. Asst. Sec: T.L. Davies.
A second Commission of 3 Apr 1897 appointed G.H. Murray in place of Milner who resigned on his appointment as Governor and Commander in Chief of the Colony of Good Hope.
**To inquire** into the present system under which taxation is raised for local purposes and report whether all kinds of real and personal property contribute equitably to such taxation, and, if not, what alterations in the law are desirable in order to secure that result. (In full.)
The first report was signed subject to reservations by Stuart-Wortley and Cripps and to a memorandum by Elliott. The second was signed with addenda by Hibbert, Murray and Cripps. J.B. Balfour did not sign and attached a note of dissent. O'Connor wrote a minority report which was partially endorsed by Stuart.
The third report was signed by Balfour of Burleigh*, Cawdor, Blair Balfour*, Hibbert, Stuart-Wortley*, Dalton, Cripps, Clare, Elliott, Smith*, Stuart* and Wharton.
*Subject to various reservations and observations.

The Chairman produced a report of Separate Recommendations partially endorsed by Blair Balfour; and with Hamilton, Murray and Stuart another separate report on Urban Rating and Site Values. Minority reports were produced by Hamilton and Murray; and O'Connor. Following publication of the third report (Cd.638) which was listed as final, the Commission issued three further reports: Cd.973, Valuation in Ireland; and separate reports for Ireland, Cd.1068; and Scotland, Cd.1067. Cd.1068 was signed subject to various observations and recommendations by the Chairman, Balfour, Hamilton, Murray, O'Connor and Stuart, while the majority and minority signatories for Cd.1067 were the same as for Cd.638.

## 95. West India 1896-98
App. 22 Dec 1896. Rep. 25 Aug 1897: 1898, C.8655, l. Other papers: 1898, C.8656-7, l; 1898, C.8669, C.8799, li. Cost not recorded. (RSM&S)
Sir H.W. Norman; Sir E. Grey; Sir D. Barbour.
Secretary: S. Olivier. (Named in Warr.)
**To inquire** into conditions and prospects of the sugar-growing West India colonies.
The chairman attached a dissent to the report.

## 96. Metropolitan Water Supplies 1897-1900
App. 1 May 1897. Rep. (1) 20 Dec 1898: 1899, C.9122, xli, 491; (2) 30 Dec 1899: 1900, Cd.25, xxxviii, Pt.1. Other papers: 1900, Cd.45, xxxviii, Pt.1; Cd.198, xxxviii, Pt.2; Cd.108, Cd.267, xxxix. Cost £3,299.
Viscount Llandaff; J.W. Mellor; Sir J.E. Dorington; Sir G.B. Bruce; A. de B. Porter; A. de C. Scott (d. 16 Oct 1899); H.W. Cripps (d. 14 Aug 1899); R. Lewis.
Secretary: C. Owen.
**To inquire** whether in regard to financial considerations and present and future water requirements it would be in the interest of ratepayers and water consumers in the metropolitan districts that the undertakings of water companies should be acquired and managed by one or several Authorities; if they are not so acquired whether local Authorities should have additional powers; the practicability of connecting any two or more of the current systems of supply, and what would be the costs of such a scheme and its legal implications.

## 97. Irish Land Acts 1897-99
App. 10 July 1897. Rep. 4 Feb 1898, C.8734, C.8859, xxxv. Appendices: 1899, C.9107, xxxiv. Cost £3,468.
Sir E. Fry; G. Fottrell; G. Gordon; A. Traill; R. Vigers.
Secretary: R.R. Cherry. (Named in Warr.)
**To inquire** into and report on the procedure, practice and methods of valuation

followed by the Land Commission and the Civil Bill Courts in Ireland under the Land Law Acts.

The publication of the Commission's findings was the subject of some controversy. Normal procedure was not to make Commission reports public until they had been presented to the House; this practice was followed in the case of the actual report, but the minutes of evidence (C.8859) were published before presentation. The Secretary made enquiries of the Press Association, the printers and the Commissioners but was unable to find out how the press had obtained the documents. His letter to Cunynghame (Assistant Under Secretary at the Home Office) of 12 March 1898 points out that Dr Traill had not answered his queries directly, and refers to correspondence between Traill and the Chairman, the contents of which were never made public. It was thus inferred that Traill was responsible for sending the documents to the Press Association. The Home Office file notes a number of possible sanctions against the Press Association, but recommended no further action unless more questions were asked in the House. (PRO.HO.45/9925/B24578)

### 98. Sewage Disposal 1898-1915

App. 7 May 1898. Rep. (1) 12 July 1901, Cd.685-6, xxxiv, Pt.1; (2) pres. 14 July 1902, Cd.1178, xlix; (3) 2 March 1903, Cd.1486-7, xxxi; (4) 28 Dec 1903: 1904, Cd.1883, xxxvii; (5) 7 Aug 1908, Cd.4278, liii, 749; (6) 9 Feb 1909, Cd.4511, xlvi, 793; (7) 16 Feb 1911, Cd.5542-3, xli; (8) 4 Nov 1912: 1912-13, Cd.6464, xlvi, 613; (9) and (10) 11 Feb 1915: 1914-16, Cd.7819-21, xxxv, 333. Other papers: 1904, Cd.1884-5, xxxvii, Cd.1886-i-iv, xxxviii; 1908, Cd.4279-80, liv; Cd.4281-2, lv; Cd.4283-6, lvi; 1913, Cd.6943, xxxix. Cost £67,887 to 31 March 1912.

Earl of Iddesleigh; Sir R.T. Thorne (d. 18 Dec 1899); C.P. Carey (d. 7 Dec 1906); C.P. Cotton; M. Foster (d. 29 Jan 1907); T.W. Harding; T.W. Killick; W. Ramsay; J.B. Russell.

Secretary: F.J. Willis. (Named in Warr.)

Subsequent Warrants of 7 Feb 1900 appointed W.H. Power in place of Thorne; 7 May 1902, T.J. Stafford in place of Cotton who resigned; 7 Jan 1907, R.A. Tatton in place of Carey; on 20 July 1910, Willis was appointed a Commissioner, and his place as Secretary taken by R.H.H. Keenlyside. Killick resigned in Sept 1901. The Commission was reappointed in a Warrant of 26 March 1910 following the death of Edward VII.

**To inquire** and report on treatment and disposal of sewage, including from industrial processes, both with regard to existing law and to the duties of Local Authorities; and to make recommendations on desirable improvements.

The ninth report was signed by Iddesleigh, Harding, Stafford, Tatton and Willis and by Ramsay and Power subject to memoranda attached. It also included a list of the members of the Commission's staff and their dates of service. The tenth and final report consists of a summary of all the previous reports.

### 99. Sierra Leone 1898-99

App. 18 June 1898. Rep. 21 Jan 1899, C.9388, C.9391, lx. Cost not recorded.
(RSM&S)
Sir D.P. Chalmers was appointed to inquire into an insurrection of natives in
Sierra Leone and generally into the state of affairs in the colony. The papers
also contain observations on the report by the Governor of Sierra Leone, Sir F.
Cardew, dated 1 May 1899.

### 100. University of London Act 1898-1900

App. 12 Aug 1898. Rep. 27 Feb 1900, Cd.83, lxvi, 57. Cost £1,487.
Lord Davey; Bishop of London; Sir W. Roberts; Sir O. Roberts; R.C. Jebb; M.
Foster; E.H. Busk.
Secretary: T.B. Saunders. (App. by separate Warr. of 23 Aug 1898.)
T. Barlow was appointed to the Commission 10 March 1899 in place of Sir W.
Roberts who resigned.
This was a Statutory Royal Commission set up to implement the Act for the
Reconstitution of the University of London (61 & 62 Vict. c.62); the
Commissioners were empowered to make statutes and regulations for the
University in general accordance with the scheme proposed by the Gresham
Commission (no. **79**) and subject to the Act, and was to continue until the end
of 1899.

### 101. Newfoundland Treaties 1898-99*

App. 31 Aug 1898. Rep. not pres.
Sir J. Bramston and Sir J.E. Erskine were appointed **to enquire** into the operation
of certain Treaties in force in Newfoundland, and to suggest measures for giving
effect to their provisions.
Secretary: Earl of Westmeath.
*No report has been traced for this Commission through either Foreign and Commonwealth Office
or Cabinet Office records, but the Treasury indexes show that it drew expenses for the salaries of the
Secretary and a servant for the Commissioners until 1899 (PRO.T.1/4559).

### 102. Accidents to Railway Servants 1899-1900

App. 30 May 1899. Rep. pres. 30 Jan 1900, Cd.41-2, xxvii. Cost £1,176.
Lord James of Hereford; Viscount Hampden; Hon. A.E. Fellowes; Sir G.E. Paget;
Sir J.W. Wolfe-Barry; Sir G.L. Molesworth; Sir A. Hickman; Sir C. Scotter; C.S.
Hutchinson; H.H.S. Cunynghame; W.M. Acworth; A.C. Elliott; J.E. Ellis; C.
Fenwick; W. Hudson.
Secretary: A.H. Higgins. (Barrister; named in Warr.)
**To enquire** into the causes of fatal and non-fatal accidents to servants of railway
companies and of truck owners; and to report on the possibility of adopting

measures to reduce them.

All signed the report with the exception of Wolfe-Barry who was unable to attend the last meeting as he was in India on business.

### 103. Salmon Fisheries 1900-02

App. 17 March 1900. Rep. 10 July 1902, Cd.1188. Other papers: Cd.1269, xiii; Cd.1280-1, xiv. Cost £4,820.

Earl of Elgin & Kincardine; Duke of Bedford; Hon. F.J. Stuart-Gray; D.N. Paton; J. Fell; W.E. Archer; C.M.P. Burn; C. Lyne; J.A. Travers.

Secretary: A.H. Higgins. (Barrister; named in Warr.)

The Commission was reappointed by Warrant of 4 March 1901 on the accession of Edward VII.

**To consider** the causes affecting the yield of salmon fisheries in England, Wales and Scotland and to report whether any change of the law was desirable.

### 104. Port of London 1900-02

App. 21 June 1900. Rep. 16 June 1902, Cd.1151, xliii. Other papers: Cd.1152, xliii; Cd.1153, xliv. Cost £4,316.

Earl Egerton; Lord Revelstoke; Hon. A. Lyttelton; Sir R. Giffen; Sir J.W. Wolfe-Barry; Sir J. Hext; J.E. Ellis.

Secretary: B. Holland.

A Warrant of 6 March 1901 appointed Revelstoke as chairman after Egerton had resigned because of ill health; W.R.W. Peel was also appointed to the Commission. The Commission was reappointed 4 March 1901 after the death of Queen Victoria.

**To inquire** into the administration of the Port of London; the adequacy of, and charges for, the accommodation and unloading of vessels; and whether any change or improvement was necessary.

### 105. South African Hospitals 1900-05

App. 24 July 1900. Rep. pres. 18 Jan 1901, Cd.453. Other papers: Cd.454, xxix; Cd.455, xxx; 1905, Cd.2440, xlvi. Cost £8,439. (RSM&S)

Sir R. Romer; Sir D. Richmond; W.S. Church; D.J. Cunningham; F. Harrison.

Secretary: Major J.T. Tennant.

**To consider** and report upon the care and treatment of the sick and wounded during the South African campaign.

This was originally appointed on 19 July 1900 as a Departmental Committee, but its status was changed to a Royal Commission in order that the Witness Protection Act (1892) would apply to the inquiry. The Act covered Royal Commissions, Statutory Inquiries and Parliamentary Committees, and while the proceedings of a Departmental Committee were held to be an occasion of qualified privilege in that 'the witness is protected unless express malice is proved against him' (G. Lushington and H.H. Asquith statement, 20 Jan 1894), this was not considered to afford sufficient protection in the present case and the Queen's permission was sought in order that a Warrant could be drawn up. (PRO.HO.45/10201/B.32430)

## 106. Arsenical Poisoning 1901-03
App. 4 Feb 1901. Rep. (1) 6 July 1901, Cd.692, ix, 283; (2) 6 Nov 1903: 1904, Cd.1848, ix, 399. Other papers: Cd.1845, Cd.1869, ix. Cost £4,418.
Lord Kelvin; Sir W.H. Dyke; T.E. Thorpe; H.C.O. Bonsor; W.S. Church; B.A. Whitelegge.
Secretary: G.S. Buchanan. (Dr of Medicine; named in Warr.)
This was the first Royal Commission appointed by Edward VII. Warrants in force at the time of Victoria's death on 22 Jan 1901 were revoked and re-issued.
**To ascertain** the amount of recent sickness and death in England and Wales resulting from arsenical poisoning in beer and other articles of food or drink; the extent to, and means by, which such poisoning was introduced; and to recommend safeguards.
Whitelegge added a memorandum to the first, and Thorpe to the second, report.

## 107. University Education in Ireland 1901-03
App. 1 July 1901. Rep. (1) 28 Sept 1901: 1902, Cd.825-6, xxxi, 21; (2) 21 Dec 1901: 1902, Cd.899-900, xxxi, 459; (3) 28 July 1902, Cd.1228-9, xxxii; (4) 28 Feb 1903, Cd.1483-4, xxxii. Cost £3,530.
Lord Robertson; Viscount Ridley; J. Healy; D.H. Madden; Sir R.C. Jebb; S.H. Butcher; J.A. Ewing; J. Rhys; A.W. Rücker; J.L. Smith; W.J.M. Starkie; W. Ward.
Secretary: J.D. Daly.
A further Warrant of 23 July 1901 appointed R.H.F. Dickey in place of Rücker who resigned.
**To inquire** into the present condition of higher, general and technical education available in Ireland, outside Trinity College, Dublin, and to report on what reforms might be needed to make that education adequate to the needs of the Irish people.
The final report was signed by all except Dickey who attached a note of dissent. Apart from Butcher all the Commissioners signed subject to various notes and reservations.

## 108. Tuberculosis 1901-11
App. 31 Aug 1901. Rep. (1) 16 May 1904, Cd.2092, xxxix, 129; (2) pres. 12 Feb 1907, Cd.3322, xxxviii; (3) pres. 16 Feb 1909, Cd.4483, xlix, 365; (4) pres. 5 July 1911, Cd.5761, xlii, 173. Other papers: 1907, Cd. 3584, xxxviii; Cd.3660, xxxix; Cd.3661, 3378, xl. 1908, Cd.3758, lvii; 1911, Cd.5790, xlii; Cd.5791, 5893, xliii; Cd.5894, 5975, xliv; 1913, Cd. 6796, 6904, xl; 1914-16, Cd.7941, xxxvii. Cost £75,615.
Sir M. Foster (d. 29 Jan 1907); G.S. Woodhead; S.H.C. Martin; J. McFadyean; R.W. Boyce.

Secretary: E.J. Steegmann.
A Warrant of 18 March 1907 appointed W.H. Power as Chairman.
**To inquire** and report with respect to tuberculosis: whether the disease was the same for humans and animals; the likelihood of reciprocal infection; and the conditions under which such cross-infection might take place.
This Commission conducted its own researches and recorded thanks to Sir J. Blyth, who allowed them the use of his farm buildings and animals for their experiments and investigations.

### 109. Coal Supply 1901-05
App. 26 Dec 1901. Rep. (1) 5 Aug 1903, Cd.1724-6, xvi; (2) 24 Feb 1904, Cd.1990-2, xxiii; (3) 7 Jan 1905, Cd. 2353-65, xvi. Cost £20,202.
W.L. Jackson (cr. Baron Allerton in 1902); Sir G.J. Armytage; Sir W.T. Lewis; Sir L. Wood; T. Bell; W. Brace; A.C. Briggs; H.B. Dixon; J.S. Dixon; C. Le Neve Foster (d. 19 Apr 1904); E. Hull; C. Lapworth; J.P. Maclay; A. Sopwith; J.J.H. Teall; R. Young (d. 17 Dec 1904).
Secretary: W. Russell. (Barrister; named in Warr.)
A Warrant of 3 Nov 1903 appointed A. Strahan as an additional commissioner.
**To inquire** into the extent and available resources of UK coalfields; their anticipated rate of exhaustion; the effect of exports on the home supply, having particular regard to the needs of the Royal Navy; the possibility of a reduction in costs; and an assessment of the competitive power of the industry.
The first report was not signed by Foster; the second was not signed by Lapworth.

### 110. Alien Immigration 1902-03
App. 21 March 1902. Rep. 10 Aug 1903, Cd.1741-3, ix. Cost £2,180.
Lord James of Hereford; Lord Rothschild; Hon. A. Lyttelton; Sir K.E. Digby; W.E. Evans-Gordon; H. Norman; W. Vallance.
Secretary: F.E. Eddis. Asst. Sec: F.W. Perrett.
**To inquire** into the nature of the evils attributed to the unrestricted immigration of aliens, especially in London; and the measures adopted by foreign countries and the British Colonies for the restriction and control of immigration.
The report was signed subject to a Memorandum by Rothschild and Digby.
In May 1904 Eddis submitted a draft pamphlet on the work of the Commission to the Home Office in which he claimed that Evans-Gordon had been appointed to attack unrestricted immigration and Rothschild to defend it and that witnesses for each side had been summoned accordingly. Despite the anger caused by Drage's book on the Labour Commission and the subsequent recommendation that Secretaries should be made aware of the responsibilities of their privileged position in order to prevent such publications in future, no definite instructions had been produced. As there was no procedure to be followed the Home Office made its usual response and referred the decision elsewhere: Eddis was advised that he should obtain the chairman's approval and the file note is that the matter should be left to Lord Hereford. (PRO.HO.45/10241/B.37811) The pamphlet does not seem to have been published, although Eddis subsequently wrote *That*

*Goldheim? A spy story, exposing a special danger resulting from alien immigration* (1918).

### 111. Physical Training in Scotland 1902-03
App. 31 March 1902. Rep. 14 March 1903, Cd.1507-8, xxx. Cost £2,368.
Earl of Mansfield; Hon. T.H.A.E. Cochrane; Sir T. Glen-Coats; Sir H. Craik; M.H. Shaw-Stewart; J.C. Alston; J.B. Fergusson; G. McCrae; A. Ogston.
Secretary: R.B. Pearson. (Advocate; named in Warr.)
**To inquire** into the state of physical training in state-aided schools and educational establishments in Scotland; and to suggest means by which such training might add to the welfare of pupils and how it might be continued for those who had left school, and thus to contribute towards the sources of national strength.

### 112. Martial Law in South Africa 1902
App. 18 Aug 1902. Rep. 28 Oct 1902, Cd.1364, lxix, 295. Cost £1,369.
Lord Alverstone; Sir J.C. Bigham; Sir J.C. Ardagh.
Secretary: G. Mellor. (Barrister; named in Warr.)
The Warrant for this Commission did not include the usual clause that the Commission should report 'from time to time'; Lord Alverstone was privately informed by the Colonial Office that they were not expected to take evidence for publication, and that only their opinion was wanted. (PRO.HO.45/10285/107553)
**To enquire** into sentences passed by the Military Courts in South Africa during the period of martial law.

### 113. Military Preparation for South African War 1902-03
App. 9 Sept 1902. Rep. 9 July 1903: 1904, Cd. 1789, xl. Other papers: 1904, Cd.1790, xl; Cd.1791, xli; Cd.1792, xlii. Cost £2,178.
Earl of Elgin & Kincardine; Viscount Esher; Sir G. Dashwood Taubmann-Goldie; Sir H.W. Norman; Sir J.O. Hopkins; Sir J. Edge; Sir J. Jackson.
Secretary: B. Holland.
A further Warrant of 11 Oct 1902 appointed Lord Strathcona & Mount Royal, and Sir F.M. Darley to the Commission.
**To inquire** into the military preparations for the War in South Africa, and into the supply of men, ammunition, equipment, and transport by sea and land in connection with the campaign, and into the military operations up to the occupation of Pretoria. (In full.)
The report was signed by all with notes by Esher, Taubman-Goldie, Darley, Edge and Jackson.

### 114. Superannuation in the Civil Service 1902-03
App. 29 Nov 1902. Rep. 10 Aug 1903, Cd. 1744-5, xxxiii, 209. Cost £466.
L.H. Courtney; Sir A. Henderson; Sir R.H. Knox; Sir W.B. Gurdon; E.W. Brabrook; J.F. Moulton; W.H. Dickinson; A.H.A. Morton; W.G. Bunn.
Secretary: L.J. Hewby. (Named in Warr.)
**To inquire** into the possibility of amending Civil Service superannuation to give

greater uniformity of advantage without increasing taxation.

The majority report was signed with notes by Henderson and Moulton; and Morton. Knox and Brabrook produced a minority report.

### 115. London Traffic 1903-05

App. 9 Feb 1903. Rep. 26 June 1905, Cd.2597, xxx, 533. Other papers: 1906, Cd.2751-2, xl-xli; Cd.2987, xlii; Cd.2798-9, xliii-xliv; Cd.2743-4, xlv-xlvi. Cost £24,490.

Sir D.M. Barbour; Earl Cawdor; Viscount Cobham; Lord Ribblesdale; Sir J.C. Dimsdale; Sir J.P. Dickson-Poynder; Sir R.T. Reid; Sir J.W. Wolfe-Barry; Sir F.J.S. Hopwood; Sir G.C.T. Bartley; C.S. Murdoch; F.O. Schuster; G.S. Gibb.

Secretary: L.L. Macassey. (Barrister; named in Warr.)

**To inquire** into means of locomotion and transport in London and to report on measures for their improvement; and on the desirability of the establishment of an authority or tribunal to which all schemes of railway or tramway construction should be referred and the powers which should be given to such an authority.

Cawdor resigned 25 March 1905 when he became First Lord of the Admiralty. Dimsdale and Gibb signed the report subject to a suppplementary report and note, respectively. Bartley did not sign and attached a separate report.

### 116. Militia and Volunteer Forces 1903-04

App. 23 Apr 1903. Rep. 20 May 1904, Cd.2061-2, xxx, 175. Cost £1,859.

Duke of Norfolk; Earl of Derby; Lord Grenfell; Sir C. Grove; Sir R.H. Knox; G. O'Callaghan-Westropp; E.H. Llewellyn; E. Satterthwaite; J.A. Dalmahoy; H.S. Wilkinson.

Secretary: H.W.W. McAnally. (Named in Warr.)

A Warrant of 15 May 1903 appointed the Earl of March (succ. as Duke of Richmond & Gordon, Sept 1903).

**To enquire** into the organization, numbers and terms of service of Militia and Volunteer Forces; and to report on any changes needed to maintain such forces in a condition of military efficiency and adequate strength.

The report was signed with memoranda by Grenfell and Westropp. Separate reports were produced by (1) Knox; (2) Satterthwaite and Dalmahoy.

### 117. Supply of Food and Raw Material in Wartime 1903-05

App. 27 Apr 1903. Rep. pres. 31 July 1905, Cd.2643, xxxix. Other papers: Cd.2644-5, xxxix-xl. Cost £3,799.

Lord Balfour of Burleigh; Prince of Wales; Duke of Sutherland; Lord Burghclere; H. Chaplin; J.L. Wharton; Sir G.H.U. Noel; Sir J.C.R. Colomb; Sir A.E. Bateman; Sir H. Seton-Karr; H.H.S. Cunynghame; E. Robertson; T.E. Holland; A. Emmott; A.S. Harvey (d. 13 March 1905); R. Montgomery; J.E. Street; J. Wilson.

Secretary: W.H. Clark. (Named in Warr.)

The Warrant names the Prince of Wales first. Uctred Noel resigned when he was appointed to the command of the China station of the Fleet, and D.H. Bosanquet was appointed to replace him by Warrant of 7 Jan 1904.

**To inquire** into conditions affecting importation of food and raw materials into Great Britain and Ireland in time of war, and into the amount of reserve supplies at any given period; and to advise on measures, in addition to the maintenance of a strong Fleet, to ensure the maintenance of supplies.

The report was signed by all members of the Commission, but subject to various reservations and memoranda by all except the Prince of Wales, the Chairman and Bosanquet.

### 118. Trades Disputes 1903-06

App. 6 June 1903. Rep. 15 Jan 1906, Cd.2825-6, lvi. Cost £2,917.

A.G. Murray (cr. Baron Dunedin, 1905); Sir W.T. Lewis; Sir G. Lushington; A. Cohen; S. Webb.

Secretary: H.B.N. Mothersole.

**To enquire** into the subject of trade disputes and trade combinations and as to the law affecting them, and to report on the law applicable to the same and the effect of any modifications thereof. (In full.)

Dunedin, Cohen and Webb signed the majority report with various notes and memoranda appended, several of which were concurred in by Lushington although he did not sign the report. He and Lewis produced separate minority reports.

### 119. Ecclesiastical Discipline 1904-06

App. 23 Apr 1904. Rep. 21 June 1906, Cd. 3040, xxxiii. Other papers: same vol., Cd.3069-70. Cost £6,168.

Sir M.E. Hicks-Beach (cr. Viscount St. Aldwyn in 1906); Archbishop of Canterbury; Marquess of Northampton; Bishop of Oxford; Sir F.H. Jeune (cr. Baron St. Helier Jan 1905); Sir J.H. Kennaway; J.G. Talbot; Sir S. Hoare; Sir E.G. Clarke; Sir L.T. Dibdin; E.C.S. Gibson (became Bishop of Gloucester in 1905); T.W. Drury; G.W. Prothero; G. Harwood.

Secretary: E.P. Charlewood.

A Warrant of 28 Apr 1905 appointed Lord Alverstone in place of St. Helier who died 9 Apr 1905.

**To inquire** into the alleged prevalence of breaches or neglect of the Law relating to the conduct of Divine Service in the Church of England and to the ornaments and fittings of churches; and to consider the existing powers and procedure applicable to such irregularities and to make such recommendations as may be deemed requisite for dealing with the aforesaid matters. (In full.)

The papers of the Commission are held at the Lambeth Palace Library, and briefly described in the Library's 1991 Annual Report, pp.23-4.

### 120. Care and Control of the Feeble-Minded 1904-08

App. 9 Sept 1904. Rep. 10 July 1908, Cd.4202, xxxix, 159. Other papers: 1908, Cd.4215-6, xxxv-xxxvi; Cd.4217-18, xxxvii; Cd.4219-20, xxxviii; Cd.4221, xxxix. Cost £19,141.

Marquess of Bath; W.P. Byrne; C.E.H. Hobhouse; F. Needham; H.D. Greene; C.E.H. Chadwyck-Healey; H.N. Burden; W.H. Dickinson; C.S. Loch; Mrs E.F.

Pinsent. Secretary: H.B.N. Mothersole. (Barrister; not named in 1st Warrant; but is in 2nd.)

Warrants of 7 Oct 1904 and 6 March 1905 appointed H.B. Donkin and J.C. Dunlop to the Commission. The Earl of Radnor became Chairman by Warrant of 25 Feb 1905 after the resignation of the Marquess of Bath. On 17 July 1906 the Commission appointed two Honorary Assistant Commissioners: Sir G.P. O'Farrell and J. Mooney.

A Warrant of 2 Nov 1906 revoked all previous Commissions and enlarged the terms of reference **to consider** the constitution, jurisdiction and working of the Commission in Lunacy and other Lunacy Authorities in England and Wales and into the expediency of amending the same or adopting some other system of supervising the care of lunatics and mental defectives; and to report as to any amendments in the law which should, in their opinion, be adopted. The personnel remained the same.

Five Commissioners, Byrne, Dickinson, Donkin, Dunlop and Mrs Pinsent, visited the USA to investigate matters there and produced a report, Cd.4221, 30 Apr 1907. Treasury officials were opposed to this visit and PRO.T.108/9326 records their hope that the proposal will not be pressed and suggests that the information sought by the Commissioners was available from the US Embassy.

The final report was signed subject to reservations by Hobhouse, Needham, Dunlop, Greene and Dickinson.

### 121. Churches in Scotland 1904-05
App. 17 Dec 1904. Rep. 12 Apr 1905, Cd.2494-5, xxiii, 113. Cost £1,005.
Earl of Elgin & Kincardine; Lord Kinnear; Sir R.W. Anstruther.
Secretary: R.A. Lee. (Advocate; named in Warr.)
**To inquire** into all the facts connected with the funds and properties held by the Free Church of Scotland and to report as to whether any action should be taken thereon by legislation or otherwise.
See also no. **123**.

### 122. Trade with South Africa 1905-06
App. 28 June 1905. Rep. 31 July 1906, Cd.3127, lvii. Other papers: Cd. 3128-9, lvii; Cd.3130-1, lviii. Cost £30,518.
Sir G. Farwell; Sir G.D. Taubman-Goldie; Sir G.S. White; Sir F. Mowatt; S.H. Morley.
Secretary: H.T. Baker.
**To inquire** into trade with South Africa in reference to allegations made in the report of the committee presided over by Lt. General Sir William Francis Butler, 22 May 1905.

### 123. Church in Scotland Act 1905-09
App. 11 Aug 1905. Counter-sealed in Edinburgh 16 Aug 1905. Rep. 23 Dec 1909: 1910, Cd.5060-1, xiii, 343. Cost £418. (LPGS)
Earl of Elgin & Kincardine; Lord Kinnear; Sir T.D. Gibson-Carmichael; Sir R.W. Anstruther; Sir C.B. Logan (d. 2 March 1907).

Secretary: R.A. Lee. (Advocate)
A Warrant of 20 Aug 1908 appointed D. Crawford. Gibson-Carmichael resigned when he was appointed Governor of the Colony of Victoria in 1908. The Commission appointed seven Assistant Commissioners: J.C. Pitman, N.K. Cochran-Patrick, J. Adam, W.A. Mackintosh, G. Moncreiff, J. Prosser and W.H. Cook.
To carry into effect the provisions of the Churches (Scotland) Act, 1905.

### 124. Motor Car Acts 1905-06
App. 2 Sept 1905. Rep. pres. 23 July 1906, Cd.3080-1, xlviii. Cost £2,455.
Viscount Selby; Marquess of Winchester; Sir D. Harrel; Sir W.B. Forwood; E.R. Henry (ktd. 1906); W.J. Mure; H.C. Monro.
Secretary: C.C. Bigham. (Captain in Army; named in Warr.)
To inquire and report as to working of the Motor Car Acts of 1896 and 1903; law and practice connected with motor cars in principal foreign countries; amendments to the Motor Car Acts and the regulations under them; the injury to roads alleged to be caused by cars; and whether there should be additional charges imposed in respect of motor cars.
The report was signed subject to a reservation from Henry and Monro.

### 125. Poor Laws 1905-09
App. 4 Dec 1905. Rep. (1) 4 Feb 1909, Cd.4499, xxxvii; (2) 14 Apr 1909, Cd.4630; (3) 13 Oct 1909, Cd.4922, xxxviii, 95. Other papers: 1909, Cd.4625-27, xxxix; Cd.4684, 4704, 4755, 4764, xl; Cd.4835-6, 4888-9, xli; Cd.4850, 4573, 4593, xlii; Cd.4653, 4690, xliii; Cd.4795, 4890, 4632, xliv; Cd.4631, 4944, xlv. Cost £53,253.
Lord G.F. Hamilton; C.O. O'Conor (d. 30 June 1906); Sir H.A. Robinson; C. Booth; Sir S.B. Provis; F.H. Bentham; A.H. Downes; T.G. Gardiner; G. Lansbury; C.S. Loch; J.P. MacDougall; T.H. Nunn; L.R. Phelps; W. Smart; H.R. Wakefield; Mrs H. Bosanquet; Mrs B. Webb; Miss O. Hill.
Secretary: R.G. Duff (LGB). Asst. Secs: J. Jeffrey (Scottish LGB); J.E. Devlin (Irish LGB); E.J.E. Craven (Statistical Dept of Customs).
A Warrant of 12 Feb 1906 appointed F. Chandler to the Commission. Rev. D. Kelly was appointed by Warrant of 30 Oct 1906 to replace the O'Conor Don. Booth resigned from the Commission early in 1908 because of ill health, but continued to receive and comment on the evidence.
To inquire into the working of the Poor Laws in the United Kingdom; and into the various ways adopted for the relief of distress outside the Poor Laws; and to advise on modification or changes in administration of Poor Laws.
PRO.HO.45/12533/134807 gives some details about the drawing up of the Warrants, and notes that 'the words "to call for information in writing" were inserted at the wish of the LGB, who want to circularize Guardians, and are anxious that there should be no doubt of their powers'.
The Commission issued three majority and three minority reports; the latter signed by Wakefield, Chandler, Lansbury and Webb. The first majority report was signed subject to memoranda by Downes; Loch and Mrs Bosanquet; Miss

Hill; and Nunn. The second, on Ireland, was signed subject to reservations or memoranda by Kelly; Robinson; Nunn; and Miss Hill. Downes signed neither the majority nor the minority report, giving as his reason his lack of knowledge of Irish affairs. The third report, on Scotland, was signed by the majority subject to reservations and memoranda by Hamilton; Downes; and Nunn.

### 126. Canals and Inland Navigation 1906-11

App. 5 March 1906. Rep. (1) 31 July 1906, Cd.3183, xxxii; (2) 31 July 1907, Cd.3716, xxxiii, Pt.1; (3) 31 July 1909, Cd.4839, xiii; (4) 4 Dec 1909: 1910, Cd.4979, xii; (5) 31 March 1911, Cd.5626, xiii, 19. Other papers: 1906, Cd.3184, xxxii; 1907, Cd.3717-18, xxxiii, Pt.1; Cd.3719, xxxiii, Pt.2; 1909, Cd.4840-1, xiii; 1910, Cd.5204, 5083, xii; 1911, Cd.5653, xiii. Cost £22,857.

Lord Shuttleworth; Lord Kenyon; Lord Brassey; Lord Farrer; Sir J.E. Dorington; Sir J.T. Brunner; Sir F.J.S. Hopwood; W.J. Crossley; R. Rea; J.F. Remnant; P. Snowden; H. Vivian; L.A. Waldron; R.C.H. Davison; J.P. Griffith; A.J. Herbertson; J.C. Inglis; H.F. Killick; J. Wilson.

Secretary: W.B. Duffield. (Barrister; named in Warr.) Asst. Sec: R.B. Dunwoody, became Secretary by Warrant of 1 Feb 1910 when Duffield resigned. G. Bray was then appointed Assistant Secretary.

The Commission appointed W.H. Lindley as Assistant Commissioner on 14 July 1906. A Commission of 8 Aug 1906 appointed M.J. Minch. Lord Kenyon resigned 23 Jan 1908 upon his election to the Board of the London and North-Western Railway Company. After the death of Edward VII on 6 May 1910 all Warrants then in force were revoked and the Commission was reappointed by Warrant of 26 May 1910 in the name of George V.

**To inquire** into the Canals and Inland Navigations of the United Kingdom and to report on their present condition and financial position; and future improvements.

The fourth report was signed subject to reservations and memoranda by Farrer, Rea, Wilson, Waldron and Killick. Remnant, Davison and Inglis each published a separate report. Farrer did not sign the final report and appended a Note stating that he could not agree to any report that sanctioned further public expenditure in Ireland unless and until a purely Irish elected assembly agreed to pay for it.

### 127. Registration of Title in Scotland 1906-10

App. 23 May 1906. Rep. 25 July 1910, Cd.5316, lviii, 67. Evidence: Cd.5357. Cost £1,444.

Lord Dunedin of Stenton; Sir S. Chisholm; C.F. Brickdale; J.S. Clark; W.J. Dundas; J.H. Finlay; N.J.D. Kennedy; R.C. Munro-Ferguson.

Secretary: J. Lamb (Advocate; named in Warr.), resigned 31 Aug 1906; replaced by F.A. Umpherston (Advocate) 1 Sept 1906.

Finlay died and a Warrant of 17 May 1907 appointed J. Prosser in his place. The Commission was reappointed by Warrant of 2 June 1910 on the accession of George V.

**To inquire** into the expediency of instituting in Scotland a system of registration of title. (In full.)

The members issued four separate reports: (1) Dunedin, Dundas and Prosser; (2) Smith, Clark and Chisholm; (3) Brickdale and Ferguson; (4) Kennedy.

### 128. Duties of Metropolitan Police 1906-08
App. 26 May 1906. Rep. 19 June 1908, Cd.4156, l. Evidence: Cd.4260-1, l-li. Cost £4,768.
A. Lyttelton; R.D. Isaacs; D.B. Jones (ktd. 1906); C.A. Whitmore; W.H. Dickinson.
Secretary: J. Leslie. Asst. Sec: J.F. Waley who replaced Leslie when he resigned.
A Warrant of 6 July 1906 appointed Brynmor Jones as Chairman in place of Lyttelton who had resigned.
To inquire into and report on the duties of the Metropolitan Police in dealing with cases of drunkenness, disorder and solicitation in the streets, and to make recommendations on the way in which such duties were discharged.
This was one of the few Commissions supported by Act of Parliament: the Metropolitan Police (Commission) Act, 22 June 1906 (6 Edw. VII c.6) gave the Commission legal powers to compel the attendance of witnesses, and the production of documents.

### 129. Trinity College and University of Dublin 1906-07
App. 2 June 1906. Rep. (1) 31 Aug 1906, Cd.3174, 3176, lvi, 601; (2) 12 Jan 1907, Cd.3311-2, xli. Cost £2,320.
Sir E. Fry; C. Palles; Sir T. Raleigh; Sir A.W. Rücker; H. Jackson; S.H. Butcher; D. Hyde; D.J. Coffey; S.B. Kelleher.
Secretary: J.D. Daly, app. 8 June 1906. (Barrister)
To inquire into and report on the present state of the two institutions, including their revenues; methods of government, systems of instruction and examination; provisions for postgraduate study and research; their place within Irish higher education; and the steps to be taken to increase their usefulness to the country.
All signed the final report but subject to a series of seven notes signed by various combinations of the Commissioners.

### 130. Mines 1906-11
App. 6 June 1906. Rep. (1) 30 May 1907, Cd.3548, xiv; (2) pres. 13 Aug 1909, Cd.4820, xxxiv, 599; (3) pres. 6 March 1911, Cd. 5561, xxxvi, 465. Other papers: 1907, Cd.3549, xiv; 1908, Cd.3873, 4349, xx; 1909, Cd.4667, 4551, 4821, xxxiv; 1911, Cd.5642, xxxvi. Cost £14,393, this includes the costs of the later Commission appointed 30 May 1910, as stated in the 1913 return. (P.P. 1913 (159), li, 765)
Lord Monkswell; Sir L. Wood; H.H.S. Cunynghame; W. Abraham; F.L. Davis; E. Edwards; T.R. Ellis; J.S. Haldane; R. Smillie.
Secretaries: S.W. Harris and G.W. Chrystal. Harris was replaced by T.E. Bettany.
Monkswell died 22 Dec 1909 and was succeeded as Chairman by Cunynghame.
A new Commission of 18 May 1907 enlarged the scope of the inquiry: to inquire and report what steps could be taken for the better prevention of

accidents in quarries. A further Commission 30 May 1910 (see no. **146**) determined the powers of the Commissioners so far as they related to Metalliferous Mines and Quarries.

**To inquire** into certain questions relating to the health and safety of miners, and the administration of the Mines Acts.

The second report was signed by all members, but with qualifying notes and memoranda from all but the Chairman. The final report was signed subject to a memorandum by Abraham.

### 131. Church in Wales 1906-10

App. 21 June 1906. Rep. 1 Nov 1910, Cd.5432-i, xiv. Other papers: 1910, Cd.5433-5, xv-xvii; Cd.5436-7, xviii; Cd.5438-9, xix. Cost £12,683.

Sir R.L.B. Vaughan-Williams; Lord H.R.H. Cecil; Sir J. Williams; F. Edwards; O. Evans; S.T. Evans; A.M. Fairbairn; J.E. Greaves; H. Jones.

Secretary: R.M. Thomas. Asst. Sec: T.H. Davies.

Thomas resigned and was replaced by F.H.M. Corbett in Oct 1909.

A Warrant of 1 May 1907 appointed Sir D.B. Jones, J.H. Davies and J.M. Gibbon in place of S.T. Evans, Fairbairn and Jones who had resigned. The Commission was revoked and reappointed by Warrant of 26 May 1910 following the accession of George V.

**To inquire** into and report on the origin, nature, amount and application of the temporalities, endowments and other properties of the Church of England in Wales and Monmouthshire; and the provision made by Churches of all denominations in Wales and Monmouthshire for the spiritual welfare of the people and the extent to which the people availed themselves of such provision. Five of the seven Commissioners who signed the report attached various qualifying notes or memoranda. Gibbon and Sir John Williams did not sign and appended memoranda giving their reasons.

### 132. Coast Erosion 1906-11

App. 6 July 1906. Rep. (1) 1 Aug 1907, Cd.3683-4, xxxiv; (2) 4 Jan 1909, Cd.4460-1, xiv, 125; (3) 31 May 1911, Cd.5708-9, xiv. Cost £11,119.

Hon. I.C. Guest (cr. Baron Ashby St. Ledgers in 1910); Sir W.H.B. ffolkes; Sir L. Lyell; W. Matthews (ktd. 1906); W.P. Beale; G.C. Frederick; H.R. Haggard; T.J. Jehu; A.L. Lever; R.B. Nicholson; P. O'Brien; T. Summerbell (d. 10 Feb 1910); A.S. Wilson.

Secretary: C.H. Grimshaw. Asst. Sec: D.R. Daniel.

A Warrant of 31 March 1908 appointed E.S. Howard, H.C. Monro, J. Galvin, W. Somerville, F. Story and J. Ward.

**To inquire** and report on the encroachment of the sea on various parts of the coast of the United Kingdom, likely damage and measures for its prevention; whether further power should be given to Local Authorities and other property owners for adoption of coastal protection schemes; the need for any alteration in the law for management of the foreshore; and whether any further facilities should be given for land reclamation.

The Commission was reappointed by Warrant of 26 May 1910 after the accession of George V. A further Warrant of 31 March 1908 extended the original terms of reference: the Commissioners were to consider whether it would be desirable to make an experiment in afforestation on reclaimed land as a means of increasing employment during periods of depression.

Howard, Monro and Story resigned after the second report was produced. This was signed subject to a reservation by Wilson; and the third report was signed subject to reservations by Nicholson, Wilson, ffolkes and Jehu.

### 133. Congestion in Ireland 1906-08

App. 20 July 1906. Rep. (1) 14 Nov 1906, Cd.3266-7, xxxii, 617; (2) 20 Nov 1906: 1907, Cd.3318-9, xxxv; (3) 23 Feb 1907, Cd.3413-4, xxxv, 333; (4) 22 Apr 1907, Cd.3508-9, xxxvi; (5) 25 June 1907, Cd.3629-30, xxxvi, 257; (6) 30 Aug 1907: 1908, Cd.3747-8, xxxix, 697; (7) 30 Sept 1907: 1908, Cd.3784-6, xl; (8) 30 Oct 1907: 1908, Cd.3838-9, xli; (9) 25 Nov 1907: 1908, Cd.3844-5, xli, 483; (10) 28 Feb 1908, Cd.4006-7, xlii; (11) 14 Apr 1908, Cd.4088-9, xlii, 583; (12) 5 May 1908, Cd.4097, xlii, 729. Other papers: 1908, Cd.4098-99, xliii. Cost £16,613.

Earl of Dudley; Sir A.P. MacDonnell; Sir J.C.R. Colomb; Sir F. Mowatt; P. O'Donnell; J.A. Bryce; W.I. Kavanagh; C. O'Kelly; A. Sutherland.

Secretary: W.E.E. Callan. (App. 24 July 1906.)

To inquire into and report on the operations of the Acts dealing with congestion in Ireland; the working of the Congested Districts Board; legal or administrative changes needed for the relief of congestion as a whole, and for bettering the condition of people living in such areas.

The final report was signed subject to reservations or notes from MacDonnell, Colomb, O'Donnell, Kavanagh and O'Kelly.

### 134. Lighthouse Administration 1906-08

App. 21 Aug 1906. Rep. 29 Jan 1908, Cd.3923, 3937, xlix, 457. Cost £1,934.

G.W. Balfour; Sir F.F. Adam; I.J.C. Herbert (ktd. 1907); W.H. Henderson; M.A. Ennis.

Secretary: C.C. Bigham. (Army Captain; named in Warr.)

To inquire into the existing system of management of the Lights, Buoys and Beacons on the coast of the United Kingdom by the three General Lighthouse Authorities, and as to the constitution and working of these Authorities, and to report on any changes which were desirable in the arrangements.

Ennis signed the report subject to a note of reservation.

### 135. Vivisection 1906-12

App. 17 Sept 1906. Rep. (1) 26 Jan 1907, Cd.3325-6, xli, 645; (2) 15 Apr 1907, Cd.3461-2, xli, 813; (3) 29 July 1907: 1908, Cd.3756-7, lvii, 279; (4) pres. 4 March 1908, Cd.3954-5, lvii, 555; (5) 28 May 1908, Cd.4146-7, lvii, 875; (6) 29 Feb 1912: 1912-13, Cd.6112-3, xlviii, 367; (7) 1 March 1912: 1912-13, Cd.6114, xlviii, 401. Cost £4,806.

Viscount Selby; A.M. Lockwood; Sir W.S. Church; Sir W.J. Collins; Sir J. McFadyean; M.D. Chalmers (ktd. 1906); A.J. Ram; W.H. Gaskell; J. Tomkinson;

G. Wilson.
Secretary: C.C. Bigham. (Named in Warr.)
Selby died 6 Nov 1909 and Ram was appointed Chairman by a Warrant of 27 Nov 1909. The Commission was reappointed by Warrant of 26 May 1910 upon the accession of George V.

**To inquire** into and report upon the practice of subjecting live animals to experiments, whether by vivisection or otherwise; and the law and its administration relating to that practice; and the desirability of any changes.

The fifth report was signed only by Selby, Lockwood, Church, Chalmers and Ram; and the final report was signed subject to reservations by Lockwood, Collins and Wilson.

### 136. Shipping Rings 1906-09

App. 29 Nov 1906. Rep. 18 May 1909, Cd. 4668, xlvii. Other papers: 1909, Cd.4669-70, xlvii; Cd.4685-6, xlviii. Cost £5,895.

A. Cohen; Earl of Jersey; Lord Inverclyde; Hon. C.N. Lawrence; Sir H. Bell; Sir W.T. Lewis; Sir F.J.S. Hopwood; Sir D.M. Barbour (repr. India); Sir A.E. Bateman; Sir J. Macdonell; R.H.M. Collins (repr. Australia); H. Birchenough (repr. South African Colonies); Hon. W.P. Reeves (repr. New Zealand); J. Barry; E.C.K. Gonner; F. Maddison; W.H. Mitchell; O.C. Philipps; O. Sanderson; A. Taylor; J. Torrance.
Secretary: J.A. Webster. (Board of Trade; named in Warr.)
Torrance resigned and a Warrant of 25 Jan 1907 appointed I.H. Mathers (repr. Canada) in his place. A further Warrant of 22 June 1907 revoked the previous Commission, reappointing all the previous members apart from the Earl of Jersey and Hopwood, and extending the terms of reference to authorise the Commissioners to make visits outside the United Kingdom for the purposes of their inquiries. This case was subsequently quoted as a precedent when the Warrants for the RC on Museums and Galleries (no. **193**) were being drawn up in order to ensure that the relevant clause about visits abroad was written into the Commission.

**To inquire** into the operation of Shipping 'Rings' or Conferences generally, and more especially into the system of deferred rebates, and to report whether such operations have caused, or are likely to cause injury to British or Colonial trade, and, if so, what remedial action, if any, should be taken by legislation or otherwise. (In full.)

The Commission produced a majority report signed by Cohen, Inverclyde, Lawrence, Bell, Lewis, Bateman, Gonner, Maddison, Mitchell, Philipps and Sanderson, subject to reservations from Inverclyde and Maddison. The minority report was signed by Barbour, Macdonell, Collins, Birchenough and Barry; with Barbour adding a reservation. Pember Reeves and Taylor signed neither report as they had been unable to attend meetings because of work and illness respectively.

### 137. Indian Decentralisation 1907-09

App. 7 Sept 1907. Rep. 25 Feb 1909*: 1908, Cd.4360, xliv. Other papers:

Cd.4361-9, xliv-xlvi. Costs: in England £17,077: in India £16,968; all costs were charged to Indian Revenues.

Sir H.W. Primrose; Sir F.S.P. Lely; Sir S.W. Edgerley; R.C. Dutt; W.S. Meyer; W.L. Hichens.

Secretary: H. Wheeler. (Indian Civil Service)

Primrose resigned and a Commission of 21 Oct 1907 appointed C.E.H. Hobhouse chairman.

**To enquire** into the current relations, for financial and administrative purposes between the supreme Government and the various Provincial Governments and other authorities in India, and to report whether those relations might be improved by decentralization.

The Chairman, Lely, Edgerley and Hichens wrote supplementary notes to the report. Dutt added footnotes at various points in the report indicating his disagreement with particular sections.

*Like the earlier RC on Oxford and Cambridge (no. **4**) the date on the report is later than the year of publication.

### 138. Whiskey and other Potable Spirits 1908-09
App. 17 Feb 1908. Rep. (1) 24 June 1908, Cd.4180-1, lviii, 415; (2) 28 July 1909, Cd.4796, xlix, 451. Other papers: 1909, Cd.4797, Cd.4876, xlix. Cost £3,108.

Lord James of Hereford; L.N. Guillemard; W.E. Adeney; J.R. Bradford; H.T. Brown; G.S. Buchanan; J.Y. Buchanan; A.R. Cushny.

Secretary: A.V. Symonds. (LGB; named in Warr.)

**To inquire** and report whether in the interests of consumers and general public health there should be restrictions on the manufacture or preparation of whiskey and other potable spirits in the United Kingdom; whether any such requirements should be extended to imported spirits; and how a uniform practice could be achieved were such protective restrictions to be imposed.

### 139. Land Transfer Acts 1908-11
App. 28 July 1908. Rep. (1) 8 Feb 1909, Cd.4509-10, xxvii, 729; (2) 19 Jan 1911, Cd.5483, Cd.5494, xxx. Cost £2,801.

Viscount St. Aldwyn; Earl Beauchamp; Lord Faber; Sir C.M. Warmington (d. 12 Dec 1908); Sir S.T. Evans; S.O. Buckmaster; D. Stewart-Smith; G. Cave; P.S. Gregory; R. Pennington (d. 13 July 1910); D.J. Shackleton; E. Wood.

Secretary: J.F. Waley. (Barrister; named in Warr.)

The Commission was reappointed by Warrant of 26 May 1910 on the accession of George V.

**To consider** and report upon the working of the Land Transfer Acts, and whether any amendments are desirable. (In full.)

### 140. Electoral Systems 1908-10
App. 31 Dec 1908. Rep. pres. 10 May 1910, Cd.5163, 5352, xxvi, 295. Cost £812.

Lord R.F. Cavendish; Lord Lochee; Hon. E.S. Montagu; Sir F.J.S. Hopwood; Sir C.P. Ilbert; Sir C.N.E. Eliot; Hon. W.P. Reeves; J.W. Hills.

Secretary: C.D. Robertson (Treasury; named in Warr.), d. 26 March 1910 before the report was completed.

**To examine** the various schemes which have been adopted or proposed, in order to secure a fully representative character for popularly elected legislative bodies: and to consider whether, and how far, they, or any of them, are capable of application in this country in regard to the existing electorate. (In full.)
Lochee signed subject to a reservation.

### 141. University Education in London 1909-13
App. 24 Feb 1909. Rep. (1) 21 Apr 1910, Cd.5165-6, xxiii, 639; (2) 2 Feb 1911, Cd.5527-8, xx; (3) 4 Oct 1911, Cd.5910-11, xx, 453; (4) 15 Dec 1911: 1912-13, Cd.6015, xxii, 581; (5) 26 June 1912: 1912-13, Cd.6311-2, xxii, 587; (6) 27 March 1913, Cd.6717-8, xl, 297. Cost £4,679 up to 31 March 1912.
R.B. Haldane; Viscount Milner; Sir R. Romer; Sir R.L. Morant; L. Currie; W.S. M'Cormick; E.B. Sargant; Mrs L. Creighton.
Joint Secretaries: J. Kemp and H.F. Heath. (Named in Warr.)
**To inquire** into the organization of the University of London and other facilities for advanced education in London for persons of either sex above secondary school age; to consider the provision for University teaching and research; and to make recommendations as to the relation between the University of London, its associated colleges and schools and the various public bodies and institutions concerned, and any desirable changes.
Reappointed 26 May 1910 after the accession of Geoge V.

### 142. Mauritius 1909-10
App. 14 May 1909. Rep. 28 Apr 1910, Cd.5185-7, xlii. Cost £2,937. (RSM&S)
Sir F.A. Swettenham; Sir E.L. O'Malley; H.B.D. Woodcock.
Secretary: A.J. Harding. (Named in Warr.)
**To investigate** and report upon the condition and resources of the Colony of Mauritius, particularly with a view to the introduction of such economies in the establishments and expenditure as might be possible without detriment to the public interests.
The chairman added a note to the report and O'Malley signed subject to his appended note of dissent.

### 143. Trade Relations 1909-10
App. 9 Aug 1909. Rep. 19 Aug 1910, Cd.5369, xi, 159. Other papers: Cd.4991, 5370-1 in same vol. Cost £3,773. (RSM&S)
Lord Balfour of Burleigh; Hon. W.S. Fielding; Hon. W. Paterson; Sir J.P. Dickson-Poynder; Sir D. Morris.
Secretary: H.R. Cowell. (Named in Warr.)
R.H. McCarthy was appointed by the Secretary of State to be an expert adviser to the Commission.
Re-appointed by Warrant of 26 May 1910 after the accession of George V.
**To report** on the commercial relations between Canada and the West Indian Colonies and steps to be taken to secure, encourage and develop mutual trading

facilities.

Poynder was created Baron Islington in 1910 when he became Governor of New Zealand, and left to take up this post before the report was signed, authorising the chairman to sign for him, and attaching a memorandum giving his views on the main subjects of the inquiry.

### 144. Selection of Justices of the Peace 1909-10

App. 5 Nov 1909. Rep. 6 July 1910, Cd.5250, 5358, xxxvii, 647. Cost £1,148.

Lord James of Hereford; Earl of Jersey; Earl of Chichester; Lord Robert Cecil; Lord Hamilton of Dalzell; Sir W.H. Dyke; H. Hobhouse; Sir F. Mowatt; Sir A.O. Williams; Sir E. Troup; F.W. Verney; J.A. Simon; W.R.D. Adkins; T.G. Ashton; W.C. Bridgeman; A. Henderson.

Secretary: A.V. Symonds. (LGB; named in Warr.)

Reappointed 26 May 1910 following the accession of George V.

**To consider and report** whether any and what steps should be taken to facilitate the selection of the most suitable persons to be Justices of the Peace, irrespective of creed and political opinion. (In full.)

Verney, Adkins and Ashton signed subject to memoranda attached. Jersey did not sign as he had been prevented from attending meetings by illness, but attached a letter expressing agreement with the report.

### 145. Divorce and Matrimonial Causes 1909-12

App. 8 Nov 1909. Rep. 2 Nov 1912: 1912-13, Cd.6478-9, xviii, 143. Other papers: Cd.6480, xix; Cd.6481-2, xx. Cost £4,443 up to 31 March 1912.

Lord Gorell; Archbishop of York; Earl of Derby; Lady F. Balfour; T. Burt; Hon. Lord Guthrie; Sir W.R. Anson; Sir L.T. Dibdin; Sir G. White (d. 11 May 1912); H.T. Atkinson; Mrs M.E. Tennant; R.D. Isaacs (ktd. 1911); E. Brierley; J.A. Spender.

Secretary: H.G. Barnes. Asst. Sec: J.E.G. de Montmorency.

The Commission was reappointed by Warrant of 26 May 1910 following the accession of George V; a further Warrant of 21 June 1910 appointed Sir F. Treves in place of Isaacs who had resigned. The Earl of Derby resigned in March 1911 and was not replaced.

**To inquire** into the present state of the law and administration thereof in divorce and matrimonial causes and applications for separation orders, especially with regard to the position of the poorer classes; and to report whether any and what amendments should be made.

The main report was signed subject to reservations by Tindal-Atkinson, Mrs Tennant and Spender. A minority report was signed by the Archbishop of York, Anson and Dibdin.

### 146. Mines and Quarries 1910-14

App. 30 May 1910. Rep. (1) 31 July 1912: 1912-13, Cd.6389-90, xli, 543; (2) 12 June 1914, Cd.7476-8, xlii, 27. Cost: see below.

Sir H.H.S. Cunynghame; R.A.S. Redmayne; J.S. Haldane; J.S. Ainsworth; R.M. Greaves; R.A. Thomas; R.T. Jones; W. Lewney; U. Lovett.

Joint Secretaries: T.E. Bettany and G. Chrystal.
**To inquire** into and report upon the health and safety of persons employed in metalliferous mines and quarries. The work of this Commission was a continuation of the previous Royal Commission into Mines and Quarries appointed 18 May 1907 and its costs were included with those of the earlier inquiry.
The final report was signed subject to memoranda by Redmayne, Jones and Lovett.

### 147. Public Records 1910-19
App. 11 Oct 1910. Rep. (1) pres. 6 Aug 1912: 1912-13, Cd.6361, xliv, 13; (2) 18 June 1914, Cd.7544, xlvi, 189; (3) 11 Apr 1918: 1919, Cmd.367, xxviii. Other papers: 1912-13, Cd.6395-6, xliv; 1914, Cd.7545-6, xlvi; 1919, Cmd.368-9. xxviii. Cost £1,478 up to 31 March 1912.
Sir F. Pollock; Sir E.V. Evans; C.H. Firth; M.R. James; F.G. Kenyon; S. Lee; H. Owen; H.R. Tedder; W.L. Williams.
Secretary: H. Hall. (PRO; named in Warr.) Asst. Sec: D. R. Daniel.
**To inquire** and report into the working of the various Public Records Acts and into matters concerning the state of the Public Records and Local Records of a public nature of England and Wales.

### 148. Malta 1911-12
App. 12 Aug 1911. Rep. 22 Apr 1912: 1912-13, Cd. 6090, xl. Other papers: Cd.6280-1, same vol. Cost £1,270. (RSM&S)
Sir F. Mowatt; R. Rea; Sir M.D. Chalmers.
Secretary: D.L.H. Baynes. (Named in Warr.)
**To inquire** into complaints concerning the Courts in Malta; and into the economic resources of the island and means whereby they might be increased or alternatively whereby occupation might be found for the unemployed of the island in other countries.

### 149. Railways Conciliation 1911
App. 22 Aug 1911. Rep. 18 Oct 1911, Cd. 5922, xxix, Pt.I., 663; Evidence: 1912-13, Cd. 6014, xlv. Cost £1,973.
Sir D. Harrel; Sir T.R. Ratcliffe-Ellis; C.G. Beale; A. Henderson; J. Burnett.
Secretary: J.J. Wills. (Bd. of Trade.)
**To investigate** the working of the Railway Conciliation and Arbitration Scheme of 6 November 1907, and to report on any desirable changes with a view to the prompt and satisfactory settlement of differences.

### 150. Civil Service 1912-15
App. 18 March 1912. Rep. (1) 2 May 1912: 1912-13, Cd.6209-10, xv, 109; (2) 21 Nov 1912: 1912-13, Cd.6534-5, xv, 255; (3) 14 March 1913, Cd.6739-40, xviii, 275; (4) 2 Apr 1914, Cd.7338-40, xvi; (5) 18 Dec 1914: 1914-16, Cd.7748-9, xi, 673; (6) 18 Nov 1915: 1914-16, Cd.7832, 8130, xii.
Lord MacDonnell; Duke of Devonshire*; Bishop of Southwark*; Sir K.A.M.

Mackenzie; Sir H. Primrose; Sir D. MacAlister*; Sir W.G. Granet; H.T. Baker; A.A. Booth*; A. Boutwood*; J.R. Clynes*; S.J.G. Hoare*; R.D. Holt*; P.E. Matheson*; A.E. Shipley*; P. Snowden*; G. Wallas*; Miss E.S. Haldane*; Mrs L.A.E. Streatfeild*.
Secretary: S. Armitage-Smith (Treasury); succ. by N.E. Behrens also of the Treasury. Behrens was appointed a Commissioner of Customs and the Treasury seconded E.W.H. Millar to replace him as Secretary.
A Warrant of 17 July 1912 appointed A.C.T. Beck in place of Baker who had resigned. MacDonnell and four of his colleagues resigned after publication of the fifth report, and a new Commission of 20 Jan 1915 appointed Sir H.B. Smith as Chairman and Sir J.P. Hewett, Sir J.A. Kempe and C. Coward as new members. The names of those members of the original Commission who retained their appointment are marked *. Further Commissions of 1 March and 18 May 1915 appointed Lord Mersey and Lord Dundas in place of Beck and Booth who had resigned; one of 25 May 1915 appointed Sir G.M. Paul an additional member. The Duke of Devonshire resigned before the completion of the final report.
To inquire into and report on the methods of making appointments to and promotions in the Civil Service, including the Diplomatic and Consular Services, and the legal departments; to investigate and recommend any advisable alterations in the system of competitive examination; and to consider whether the existing arrrangements met the needs of the Public Service and suggest any necessary modifications.
The fourth report was divided: the majority report was signed subject to reservations by all the signatories apart from the Chairman; the minority report was signed by Primrose, Granet and Booth. The fifth report was signed subject to reservations by Primrose, Beck, Booth, Boutwood, Clynes, Holt, Wallas Mrs Streatfeild; and a dissent from Hoare. Snowden was out of the country and thus unable to sign the report, and Granet had resigned from the Commission before the report was completed. The final report was signed subject to reservations by Southwark, Dundas, Hoare, Hewett, Boutwood, Clynes, Holt, Snowden, Wallas and Mrs Streatfeild. PRO.T.100/1-2 contain minutes and correspondence.

## 151. Natural Resources 1912-17
App. 15 Apr 1912. Rep. (1) 28 Dec 1912: 1912-13, Cd.6515, xvi, 91; (2) 16 Jan 1914, Cd.7210, xviii, 137; (3) 25 June 1914, Cd.7505, xviii, 447; (4) 9 Dec 1914: 1914-16, Cd.7711, xiv; (5) 31 Jan 1917: 1917-18, Cd.8457, viii, 159; (6) 21 Feb 1917: 1917-18, Cd.8462, x. Other papers: 1912-13, Cd.6516-7, xvi; 1914, Cd. 7170-2, xvii; Cd.7173, Cd.7351, xviii; 1914-16, Cd.7706-7, Cd.7710, xiii; Cd. 7898, Cd.7971, Cd.8123, Cd.8156, xiv; 1917-18, Cd.8458, viii; Cd.8459-61, ix. Lord Inchape (resigned 22 Aug 1912*); Sir E. Vincent (cr. Baron D'Abernon of Esher 2 July 1914); Sir C.J. Owens; Sir H.R. Haggard; T. Garnett; W. Lorimer (ktd. Feb 1917): all repr. United Kingdom; Hon. G.E. Foster, repr. Canada (ktd. 22 June 1914); D. Campbell, repr. Australia; Sir J.G. Ward, repr. New Zealand; Sir D.P. de V. Graaff, repr. Union of South Africa; E.R. Bowring, repr. Newfoundland (ktd. 18 June 1915).
Secretary: W.A. Robinson (Colonial Office; named in Warr.); succ. by E.J.

Harding in Warr. of 17 Nov 1912. Asst. Sec: W.J. Glenny.
Further Commissions: 5 July 1912, J.R. Sinclair and Sir R. Solomon appointed
to succeed Ward and de Graaff; 31 Aug 1912, A. Morley to succeed Inchape; 15
Nov 1912, J. Tatlow succ. Owens; 17 Nov 1912, Sir A.E. Bateman succ. Morley.
Vincent became Chairman on 26 Nov 1912. A new Commission was issued on
24 Feb 1913 recording these changes. Solomon died 10 Nov 1913 and was
replaced by Sir J.W.S. Langerman in a Commission of 12 Feb 1914.
The Commission came into being as a result of a resolution passed at the
Imperial Conference of 1911 (Cd.5745, 1911, liv, 103): **to enquire** into and
report upon the natural resources of Canada, Australia, New Zealand, South
Africa and Newfoundland; their development; facilities for production and
distribution of commerce; their requirements of food and raw materials, and also
of those of the United Kingdom; their trade with one another, the United
Kingdom and the rest of the world; the extent to which laws other than fiscal
laws affect such trade; and to suggest any methods by which such trade might
be extended and improved, consistent with the existing fiscal policy of each part
of the Empire.
The Commission sat for five years, largely because its proceedings were
interrupted by war, and the final report was signed by D'Abernon, Rider
Haggard, Garnett, Lorimer, Tatlow, Bateman, Foster, Sinclair, Langerman and
Bowring.

*Inchape's resignation only four months from the appointment of the Commission was officially
described as due to business commitments. However his chairmanship had been opposed by
Unionist MPs because of his strong free trade views, and there had been a number of Parliamentary
questions concerning his suitability for the post.

## 152. Fuel and Engines 1912-14
App. 31 July 1912. Rep. (1) 27 Nov 1912; (2) 27 Feb 1913; (3) 10 Feb 1914. No
Command numbers; the reports were marked 'subject to the provisions of the
Official Secrets Act', stamped 'Secret', and were not presented to Parliament.
Copies of the reports, evidence and other papers are held at the PRO in
ADM.116/1208-9 and ADM.265/32-38.
Lord Fisher; G. Lambert; Sir B. Redwood; Sir P. Watts; Sir H.J. Oram; Sir J.R.
Jellicoe; Sir W. Matthews; Sir T.H. Holland; Sir T.E. Thorpe; A. Gracie; H.O.
Jones; A.F. Yarrow.
Secretaries: P.W. Dumas; C.J. Hawkes; J.H. Narbeth. Dumas was subsequently
appointed to H.M.S. *Roxburgh* and succeeded as Secretary by Captain S.S. Hall.
(All were naval personnel.)
Although the Commission reports were not made public, the Warrants were
drawn up in the usual way and printed in the *London Gazette*. A further Warrant
of 8 Sept 1912 appointed G.T. Beilby in place of Jones who died. Vice-Admiral
Jellicoe was appointed Second Sea Lord and his place on the Commission was
taken by Sir R.F.H. Henderson by Warrant of 18 Feb 1913.
**To report** on the means of supply and storage of Liquid Fuel in peace and war,
and its application to warship engines, whether indirectly or by internal
combustion. (In full.)
The first and second reports were signed subject to notes of reservation by

Lambert, who dissented from his colleagues over their recommendations for the minimum requirements for the storage of oil supplies. Their recommendation for the storage of four years' supply was based on peacetime consumption; Lambert wanted estimates based on war-time consumption, and also stressed the need to retain and maintain coal supplies.

### 153. Public Services (India) 1912-15
App. 31 Aug 1912. Rep. 14 Aug 1915: 1916, Cd.8382, vii, 87. Other papers: 1914, xxi-xxiv; 1914-16, xv-xvii. (19 Cd. papers)
Lord Islington; Earl of Ronaldshay; Sir M. Hammick; Sir T. Morison; Sir V. Chirol; M.B. Chaubal; A. Rahim; G.K. Gokhale (d. 19 Feb 1915); W.C. Madge; F.G. Sly; H.A.L. Fisher; J.R. Macdonald.
Joint Secretaries: M.S.D. Butler (Indian Civil Service) and R.R. Scott (Adm.).
Assistant Commissioners are listed in Appendix IV of the report.
To examine and report on a wide range of matters connected with the Indian Civil Service and generally to consider the requirements of the Public Service, and to recommend such changes as might seem expedient.
Apart from the Chairman all members signed subject to various attached notes.

### 154. Housing of Industrial Population of Scotland 1912-17
App. 30 Oct 1912. Rep. 11 Sept 1917: 1917-18, Cd.8731, 8760, xiv, 345.
Sir H. Ballantyne; Lord Lovat; Sir W. Younger; W.F. Anderson; G.F. Barbour; C. Carlow; J.F. Duncan; D. Gilmour; J.M. Henderson; W.L. Mackenzie; J. Middleton; Mrs H.L. Kerr.
Secretary: P.G. Gillespie. Asst. Sec: A. M'Kinna.
Anderson died and was replaced by Rev. J. Barr by Warrant of 22 Feb 1915.
To inquire into the Housing of the Industrial Population of Scotland, rural and urban (with special reference in rural districts to the Housing of Miners and Agricultural Labourers), and to report what legislative or administrative action is, in their opinion, desirable to remedy existing defects. (In full.)
The Commission appointed J. Wilson as a Special Investigator and his report on the design of various types of housing was issued as Cd.8760 (above).
The Commission's work was suspended in Feb 1916 on the instructions of the Treasury and the Secretary for Scotland because of the War. Sittings were resumed in Jan 1917, and majority and minority reports were produced; the latter signed by Lovat, Barbour, Carlow and Mrs Kerr, and subject to reservations by Barbour and Carlow.

### 155. Delay in the King's Bench Division 1912-13
App. 31 Dec 1912. Rep. (1) pres. 18 Apr 1913, Cd.6761-2, xxx, 683; (2) 28 Nov 1913: 1914, Cd.7177-8, xxxvii.
Viscount St. Aldwyn; Viscount Goschen; Sir C.J. Darling; Sir C.S. Henry; Sir E.A. Cornwall; R.B.D. Acland; C. Coward; H.J. Craig; C.H. Morton; G.H. Roberts; S. Roberts.
Secretary: J.F.T. Atkinson.
To enquire into the complaints of delay in the hearing of actions and appeals

and Crown Cases in the King's Bench Division of the High Court of Justice, and whether any reforms should be adopted, and to report thereupon. (In full.)
The second report was signed subject to a Note by Morton.

### 156. Indian Finance and Currency 1913-14
App. 17 Apr 1913. Rep. (1) 6 Aug 1913: 1914, Cd.7068-9, xix, 507; (2) 24 Feb 1914, Cd.7236, xx, 709. Other papers: same vol., Cd.7070-2; Cd.7237-9.
J.A. Chamberlain; Lord Faber; Lord Kilbracken; Sir R. Chalmers; Sir E. Cable; Sir S.B. Broacha; Sir J. Begbie; R.W. Gillan; H.N. Gladstone; J.M. Keynes.
Secretary: B.P. Blackett. (Treasury)
**To inquire** into and make recommendations upon the location and management of the general balances of the Government of India and related financial matters. The final report was signed subject to a Note by Begbie.

### 157. Railways 1913-15
App. 24 Oct 1913. No Report recorded.
Earl of Loreburn; Earl of Derby; F.H. Jackson; Sir H.W. Primrose; Sir F.R. Upcott; Sir W. Plender; R.E. Prothero; D.J. Shackleton.
Secretary: E.W. Rowntree. Asst. Sec: M.L. Chute. (Both of Bd. of Trade.)
**To inquire** into the relationship between the Railway Companies of Great Britain and the State in respect of matters other than safety of working and conditions of employment, and to report what changes, if any, are desirable in that relationship. (In full.)
*The Times* of 24 Oct 1913 gave brief biographies of the Commissioners, and background information on the Commission, referring to the previous inquiry in 1865 (see Collinge, no. 111), and noted that apart from Sir F. Upcott, who had previously been Chairman of the Board of Indian Railways, none of the Commissioners had any railway experience.
It seems that the Commission's activities were interrupted because of the war, and were not resumed. It continued to hear evidence until 1915; a letter to the Treasury from H.L. Smith, Permanent Secretary at the Board of Trade (3 Feb 1915) noted that fifty-eight witnesses had been examined up to that date (PRO.T.1.11833/23835). On 12 Feb 1915 the allowance to the Secretary was discontinued; and the Assistant Secretary was paid a reduced allowance of £100 per annum (PRO.T.108/4318).

### 158. Venereal Diseases 1913-16
App. 1 Nov 1913. Rep. (1) 8 June 1914, Cd.7474-5, xlix, 109; (2) 11 Feb 1916, Cd.8189-90, xvi.
Lord Sydenham of Combe; Sir D.B. Jones; Sir K.E. Digby; Sir A.W. Fitzroy; Sir M.A. Morris; Sir J. Collie; A. Newsholme; J.W. Horsley; J.S. Lidgett; F.W. Mott; Mrs M.D. Scharlieb; J.E. Lane; P. Snowden; Mrs L. Creighton; Mrs E.M. Burgwin.
Secretary: E.R. Forber. (LGB)
**To inquire** into the prevalence of Venereal Diseases in the United Kingdom, their effects upon the health of the community, and the means by which those

effects can be alleviated or prevented, it being understood that no return to the policy or provisions of the Contagious Diseases Acts of 1864, 1866 or 1869 is to be regarded as falling within the scope of the inquiry. (In full.)
The final report was signed subject to notes by Digby and Horsley.

### 159. Meat Export Trade of Australia 1914
App. 5 June 1914. Rep. 14 Nov 1914: 1914-16, Cd.7896, xlvi.
P.W. Street was appointed **to inquire** into and report as to the operations of any person, combination or trust tending to create any restraint of trade or monopoly in connexion with the export of meat from Australia. (In full.)
Secretary: W.H. Clarke, succ. by S.F. Chubb.
The Warrant was issued by Letters Patent under the Commonwealth Seal in the name of the King by the Governor General of Australia. The report is a document of the Commonwealth of Australia, but was presented to the United Kingdom Parliament as a Royal Commission.

### 160. Landing of Arms at Howth 1914
App. 5 Aug 1914. Rep. 4 Sept 1914: 1914-16, Cd.7631, 7649, xxiv, 805.
Lord Shaw; T.F. Molony; W.D. Andrews.
Secretary: A. Shaw.
**To enquire** into and report upon the events connected with and ensuing upon the recent landing of arms at Howth, including the circumstances in which the Military were requisitioned to assist the civil power in the City of Dublin, and the origin and character of the disturbances which occurred. (In full.)

### 161. Sugar Supply 1914-21
App. 20 Aug 1914. Rep (1) 22 Dec 1916: 1917-18, Cd.8728, xviii, 633; (2) pres. 13 May 1921, Cmd.1300, xviii, 709. Other papers: 1916, Cd.8395, xxiv, 537; 1919, Cd.447, xxxii; 1920, Cmd.1069, xxv.
R. McKenna; Lord Lucas; W. Runciman; Sir H.W. Primrose; Hon. E.S. Montagu; G.S. Barnes (ktd. 1915); R.P. Lyle; W.C. Slaughter.
Secretary: C.S. Rewcastle; succ. as Secretary and Manager by J.J. Runge.
The Commission was appointed by Order in Council, but Warrants were drawn up and issued in the usual way. The ministerial members (McKenna, Runciman and Montagu) resigned when the Government changed in Dec 1916 and Warrants of 24 Jan 1917 appointed Lord Devonport, G.E. May and A. Taylor. On 27 March 1916, H. Fountain was appointed to replace Barnes who had resigned; Sir J. White-Todd was appointed 25 Apr 1917; and Sir A.G. Anderson on 11 Oct 1918.
**To enquire** into the supply of sugar in the United Kingdom; to purchase, sell and control the delivery of sugar on behalf of the Government, and generally to take steps to maintain the supply.
The Commission became a section of the Ministry of Food (cr. 1916) in 1917 and Lord Devonport, the Food Controller, became Chairman. Sir Charles Bathurst (cr. Baron Bledisloe 1918) was appointed Chairman by Warrant of 14 Aug 1917 after the retirement of Lord Devonport. He resigned in Nov 1920 and

Primrose became Chairman. Primrose had been the effective Chairman since Lord Devonport's resignation as Food Controller as he made clear in the letter accompanying his memorandum on the status of the Royal Commission (Primrose to Ministry of Food, 30 July 1917). In a further letter to the new Food Controller, Lord Rhondda (24 Oct 1917) Primrose recorded that all the unofficial members of the Commission took strong exception to the suggestion that the work of the Royal Commission should be under the direction of the Food Controller. However this Commission, and those subsequently appointed to oversee the supplies of paper and wheat, eventually took on an administrative rather than a purely advisory role, with a number of sub-committees and a large staff. Some staff records have been retained in PRO.MAF.60/289-90. See also Appendix 2.

### 162. Defence of the Realm 1915-20
App. 31 March 1915. Rep. (1) 19 Sept 1916, Cd.8359, vii; (2) 20 Sept 1917: 1917-18, Cd.8751, x, 485; (3) 10 Oct 1918, Cd.9181, viii, 35; (4) 28 Oct 1919, Cmd.404, xiii, Pt.1, 905; (5) 10 Nov 1920, Cmd.1044, xiii, 861. Other papers: 1918, Cd.9048, viii.
H.E. Duke; Sir J.T. Woodhouse (cr. Baron Terrington, Jan 1918); Sir M.G. Wallace.
Secretary: H.E. Dale (Development Commission); succ. by D.D. Davidson (Bd. of Education) in Oct 1915.
The Commission was reconstituted by an Order in Council of 2 Aug 1915. A Warrant of 12 Sept 1916 appointed E. Shortt, with Woodhouse as Chairman in place of Duke who had resigned. Warrants of 29 Sept 1917 and 20 March 1918 appointed L. Hardy and W.F. Hamilton as additional members. The Hon. W. Watson was appointed by Warrant of 25 June 1918 to replace Shortt who resigned following his appointment as Chief Secretary for Ireland. These appointments were confirmed in a new Commission with extended terms of reference issued on 18 Dec 1918. Terrington and Hardy resigned in 1920, and the final report was signed only by Wallace, Hamilton and Watson. A Warrant of 8 Sept 1920 reconstituted the Commission as the War Compensation Court, appointing Sir A.T. Lawrence as President; and Lord Hunter as President in the case of Scottish claims. The remaining members of the original Commission were re-appointed and were joined by Sir D.P. Barton and Sir W.F.K. Taylor as additional members.
**To inquire** and determine, and to report what sums (in cases not otherwise provided for) ought in reason and fairness to be paid out of public funds to United Kingdom applicants in respect of substantial loss or damage through the exercise by the Crown of its rights and duties in defence of the Realm.

### 163. Paper Supply 1916-18
App. 15 Feb 1916. Reports included with those of the Paper Industry Committee.
Sir T.P. Whittaker; Sir A. Spicer; Sir W.R. Nugent; Sir F. Macmillan; Sir R. Bailey; G. Brown; W.H. Hazell; J. Jeremiah; E. Parke; O. Partington; A. Reed.
Secretary: J.S. Clemons. Asst. Sec: R. Benyon.

Whittaker resigned and Sir H. Birchenough took his place as Chairman by a
Warrant of 2 June 1917 which appointed L. Evans to replace Partington who had
also resigned. A Warrant of 8 Aug 1917 added A. Spurgeon to the Commission.
**To issue** licences and arrange for the importation and distribution of
paper-making materials; the terms extended to regulate United Kingdom
production of such materials by the Warrant of 2 June 1917.
The Commission was dissolved by the King on 8 March 1918 and its work and
some of its personnel incorporated into the Paper Industry Committee, chaired by
Sir H.A. Vernet, the Controller of Paper. (PRO.BT.13/85/E.35411,
BT.13/94/E.38389)

### 164. University Education in Wales 1916-18
App. 12 Apr 1916. Rep. (1) 8 March 1917: 1917-18, Cd.8500, 8507, xii; (2) 20
July 1917: 1917-18, Cd.8698-9, xii, 337; (3) 6 Feb 1918, Cd.8991, 8993, xiv.
Viscount Haldane; Hon. W.N. Bruce; Sir W. Osler; Sir H. Jones; Sir O.M.
Edwards; W.H. Bragg; W.H. Hadow (ktd. 1918); A.D. Hall; Miss E. Penrose.
Secretary: A.H. Kidd. (Bd. of Education)
**To enquire** into the organization and work of the University of Wales and its
three constituent Colleges and their relations with other institutions in Wales
providing post-secondary education and to consider possible improvements and
changes in the constitution, functions and powers of the University and its
Colleges.
T.1/11948/19301/16 gives considerable detail about the background to this
Commission.

### 165. Rebellion in Ireland 1916
App. 10 May 1916. Rep. 26 June 1916, Cd.8279, 8311, xi, 171.
Lord Hardinge of Penshurst; Sir M. Shearman; Sir M.D. Chalmers.
Secretary: E.G. Mears. (The report notes that his appointment was honorary.)
**To enquire** into the causes of the recent outbreak of rebellion in Ireland, and into
the conduct and degree of responsibility of the civil and military executive in
Ireland in connection therewith. (In full.)

### 166. Arrest and Subsequent Treatment of Mr F.S. Skeffington, Mr T. Dickson and Mr P.J. McIntyre 1916
App. 17 Aug 1916. Rep. 29 Sept 1916, Cd.8376, xi, 311.
Sir J.A. Simon; T.F. Molony; D.S. Henry.
Secretary: H.L. Murphy.
**To inquire** into and report upon the facts and circumstances connected with the
treatment of the above-named upon and after their arrest on 25 Apr 1916.

### 167. Wheat Supplies 1916-25
App. 10 Oct 1916. (1) Rep. 31 Aug 1921, Cmd.1544, xviii, 809; (2) 4 July 1925:
1924-25, Cmd.2462, xv, 1103.
Earl of Crawford; Sir A.G. Anderson; Sir R.H. Rew; Sir E.G. Saltmarsh; T.
Royden (ktd.1919); J.F. Beale; H.W. Patrick; H. Rathbone; O. Robinson.

Joint Secretaries: H.D. Vigor (Bd. of Agriculture) and Captain F. Elliot (subsq. app. Freight Manager); Vigor was sole Secretary from 1916.

An order in Council of 27 Oct 1916 and a Warrant 25 Apr 1917 extended the Commission's terms of reference, and on 1 Nov 1917 it became an administrative division of the Ministry of Food. There were many changes in membership and a complete list of all subsequent members is included in the second report. Further details of its staff and activities are given in PRO classes MAF.60 and BT.13.

**To inquire** into the supply of wheat and flour in the United Kingdom; to purchase, sell and control the delivery of wheat and flour on behalf of His Majesty's Government; and generally to take such steps as may seem desirable for maintaining the supply. (In full.)

A Warrant of 9 Dec 1921 restricted the terms of reference, and the personnel of the Commission was reduced to twelve: the Chairman; Saltmarsh; Royden; and Sir W. Mitchell-Thomson (Vice-Chairman); Sir H.J. Forde; Sir H. Gibson; R.A. Love; Sir W.P. Burton; Sir A.W. Holmes; F.H. Coller; A.W. Hurst; H.M. Taylor. The Secretary was G.E. Scarffe. Subsequently the numbers were further reduced to the Chairman, Vice-Chairman, Coller, Hurst and Taylor, who were charged with winding up the affairs of the Commission, and who signed the second report.

### 168. Allegations against Sir John Jackson, Limited 1916-17

App. c.16 Nov 1916. Rep. 30 March 1917: 1917-18, Cd.8518, xv, 189.
Sir A.M. Channell; Sir F. Crisp; Sir A.R. Stenning.
Secretary: H.G. Bushe.

**To inquire** into the allegations made against Sir John Jackson Limited in the second report of the Public Accounts Committee (115, 8 Aug 1916).

Sir J. Jackson MP was head of one of the largest public works contractors of the time, which had undertaken work for British and foreign governments. The Royal Commission had been requested by Jackson following the publication of the Public Accounts Committee report which suggested that he had abused his position by offering to erect army huts without profit in order to obtain an inordinate amount of commission for later work. The Commission's report exonerated Sir John or his company from having brought about a situation in which they could demand large payments, since the government could have placed subsequent work with another contractor, but concluded that the amount claimed for the later work was excessive and inconsistent with his earlier profession of patriotic motives.

### 169. Proportional Representation 1918

App. 25 Feb 1918. Rep. 30 Apr 1918, Cd.9044, viii, 603.
J.W. Lowther; Hon. Lord Dundas; Sir T.H. Elliott; Sir S.B. Provis; Sir W.T. Jerred.
Joint Secretaries: A.E. Wood and G.W.B. McLeod.
Assistant Commissioners: A.O.M. Mackenzie; A.B. Lowry; P.H. Bagenal; R.C. Maxwell; J.W. Thompson; H.R. Williams.

Appointed under sub-section (2) of section 20 of the Representation of the People Act, 1918, to prepare a scheme under which as nearly as possible one hundred members should be elected to the House of Commons at a General Election on the principle of proportional representation for constituencies in Great Britain returning three or more members.

## 170. Decimal Coinage 1918-20
App. 26 Aug 1918. Rep. 23 Feb 1920, Cmd.628, 719, xiii, 467.
Lord Emmott; Lord Southwark; Lord Faber (resigned at the beginning of the inquiry); Lord Ashton of Hyde; Lord Leverhulme; Sir R.V. Vassar-Smith; Sir J. Larmor; Sir G.C. Marks; Sir A.W. Watson; J.W. Cawston; S. Armitage-Smith; C. Godfrey; J. Bell; J. Burn; H. Cox; G. Hayhurst; T. McKenna; G. Marks; J.F. Mason; G.M. Smith (d. 18 Apr 1919); G.C. Vyle.
Secretary: H.E. Fass.
**To consider** and report whether it was advisable to make any changes in the denomination of the currency and money of account of the United Kingdom with a view to placing them on a decimal basis.
The main report was signed by thirteen Commissioners with reservations from Ashton and Godfrey. Minority reports were produced by (1) Southwark, Cox, McKenna and Vyle; (2) Leverhulme, Hayhurst and Smith.

## 171. Income Tax 1919-20
App. 4 Apr 1919. Rep. 11 March 1920, Cmd.615, xviii, 97. Other papers: 1919, Cmd.288-i-viii, xxiii, Pts. 1 & 2; 1920, (71) xxvii.
Lord Colwyn; Sir T.P. Whittaker (d. 9 Nov 1919); C.W. Bowerman; W. Brace; E.G. Pretyman; Sir E.E. Nott-Bower; Sir J.S. Harmwood-Banner; Sir W. Trower; R.M. Holland-Martin; N.F.W. Fisher; S. Armitage-Smith; P. Birley; W. Graham; A. Hill (d. 23 Oct 1919); D.M. Kerly; Mrs L.C.A. Knowles; H.J. Mackinder; W. McLintock; E. Manville; G. Marks; H.J. May; A.C. Pigou; N.J. Synnott.
Secretary: E. Clark. Asst. Sec: H.M. Sanders.
Warrants of 1 May and 30 Aug 1919 appointed J.W. Clark and J.C. Stamp as additional members; and of 31 Oct 1919 appointed H.A. Trotter in place of Hill who resigned. Mackinder resigned upon his appointment as High Commissioner for South Russia. In Feb 1920 Armitage-Smith took up an official position in Persia and did not sign the report.
**To inquire** into the income-tax (including super-tax) of the United Kingdom in all its aspects, including the scope, rates and incidence of the tax; allowances and reliefs; administration, assessment, appeal and collection; and prevention of evasion; and to report what alterations of law and practice are necessary or desirable and what effect they would have on rates of tax if it were necessary to maintain the total yield. (In full.)
Only Colwyn, Trower, Holland-Martin, Birley, Kerly, Manville and Trotter signed the report unreservedly. The other members all signed subject to various reservations and memoranda. Dr Knowles signed three - the most substantial of which was to recommend the separation of husband and wife's income for tax.

**172. Coal Industry 1919**
App. 26 Feb and 26 Apr 1919. Rep. 20 March 1919, Cmd.84-6; Cmd.359, xi; (2) 20 June 1919, Cmd.210, xi; Cmd.360, xii; Cmd.361, xiii, pt.1.
Sir J. Sankey; Sir A.M. Duckham; Sir A.M. Smith; Sir L.C. Money; A. Balfour; R.W. Cooper; J.T. Forgie; F. Hodges; R. Smillie; H. Smith; R.H. Tawney; S. Webb; E. Williams.
Assessors: Sir R.A.S. Redmayne; H.J. Wilson; S.J. Chapman.
Secretary: A.D. McNair. Asst. Sec: G. Stone.
A Warrant of 8 May 1919 appointed Sir A. Nimmo in place of Forgie who resigned.
The Commission was appointed under the terms of the Coal Industry Commission Act, 26 Feb 1919 (9 Geo. V c.1) **to inquire** into the position of, and conditions prevailing in, the coal industry. The Act lists the areas of inquiry and the powers of the Commissioners; these were incorporated into the Royal Warrants issued on 26 Apr 1919 after the Commission's first report.

**173. Agricultural Industry in Great Britain 1919**
App. 15 July 1919. Rep. 10 Dec 1919, Cmd.473, viii (interim report only, final report not published). Other papers: Cmd.345, 365, 391, and 445 in same vol; 1920, Cmd.665, ix.
Sir W.B. Peat; Sir W.J. Ashley; C.M. Douglas; G.G. Rea; W.A. Simmons; H. Overman; A.W. Ashby; A. Batchelor; H.S. Cautley; G. Dallas; J.F. Duncan; W. Edwards; F.E. Green; J.M. Henderson; T. Henderson; T.P. Jones; E.W. Langford; R.V. Lennard; G. Nicholls; E.H. Parker; R.R. Robbins; W.R. Smith; R.B. Walker.
Joint Secretaries: A. Goddard and R.S. Langford.
**To inquire** into the economic prospects of the agricultural industry in Great Britain, with special reference to the adjustment of a balance between prices of agricultural commodities, the costs of production, the remuneration of labour, and hours of employment. (In full.)
The Commission produced a majority and a minority report. Cautley signed the former subject to a reservation, and also attached a dissent to several of its recommendations. The minority report was signed by Ashby, Dallas, Duncan, Edwards, Green, both Hendersons, Jones, Lennard, Smith and Walker.

**174. Oxford and Cambridge 1919-22**
App. 14 Nov 1919. Rep. 1 March 1922, Cmd.1588, Sess.I, x, 27.
H.H. Asquith; Lord Ernle; Lord Chalmers; G.W. Balfour; Sir J.A. Simon; A. Henderson; Hon. E.G. Strutt; T.B. Strong (became Bishop of Ripon 1920); Sir H. Frank; Sir W.M. Fletcher; Sir H. Darwin; Sir H.A. Miers; Sir J.H. Oakley; W.H. Bragg (ktd. 1920); G.M. Trevelyan; Miss E. Penrose; W.G.S. Adams; H.K. Anderson; Miss B.A. Clough; H.M. Cobb; M.R. James; A. Mansbridge; A. Schuster (ktd. 1920).
Secretary: C.L. Stocks. (Treasury)
The Commission was divided into three sub-committees which were listed in the Warrant: (1) Oxford: Chairman, Asquith; Secretary, M.N. Tod; (2) Cambridge: Chairman, Balfour; Secretary, E. Bullough; (3) Estates Management: Chairman,

Ernle; Secretary, C.B. Marshall.

A subsequent Warrant appointed W. Graham in place of Henderson who had resigned.

To consider the applications made by the Universities of Oxford and Cambridge for financial assistance from the State and for this purpose to enquire into and make recommendations upon various matters connected with their finance and administration.

Miss Clough, Darwin and Graham attached notes of reservation to the main report.

### 175. University of Dublin & Trinity College, Dublin 1920

App. 10 March 1920. Rep. 12 Nov 1920, Cmd.1078, xiii, 1189. Evidence: 1921, Cmd.1167, xi. Cost £254.

Sir A. Geikie; Sir J. Ross; A.E. Shipley; J.S.E. Townsend; J. Joly.

Secretary: G. Waterhouse. (Professor of German at University of Dublin; named in Warr.)

**To consider** the application made by the University of Dublin for financial assistance from the State, and to enquire into, and make recommendations upon, the financial resources, administration and constitution of the University and of Trinity College.

### 176. Fire Brigades 1921-23

App. 19 Jan 1921. Rep. 20 July 1923, Cmd.1945, xi, 167. Evidence: Non P.P., HO, 1922. Est. cost £3,081.

Hon. Sir P.M. Laurence; Sir J.E. Petavel; Sir S. Sladen; Sir V.H.P. Caillard; Sir M. Fitzmaurice; A.L. Dixon; G. Symonds; V.L. Henderson; J.T. Burns; H. Peters; H.E. Stilgoe.

Secretary: J.C. MacIver. (Home Office)

Further Warrants of 2 Feb 1921 added F. Caldwell, C.F. De Salis, R. M'Connell, and of 11 Apr 1921 D.L. Solomon to the Commission. Caillard resigned 31 May 1921, due to lack of time to attend meetings, and was not replaced.

**To inquire** into existing provision for (1) the avoidance of loss from fire and (2) the extinction of outbreaks of fire, due regard being paid to considerations of economy as well as of efficiency.

All signed the report but only Petavel and Henderson signed without adding reservations.

Treasury files contain considerable amounts of detail about this Commission, largely concerning their efforts to block it. They considered the Home Office had 'behaved very badly about the appointment of this Royal Commission'; neither the terms of reference nor the personnel, nor the estimated cost had been approved by the Treasury. The Home Office had sought to justify this omission on the grounds that the Commission had been decided upon before receipt of a Treasury Circular (F.2355, 17 Dec 1920) which required Treasury sanction for committees which were likely to involve considerable expenditure; but 'the necessity for economy did not start with this Treasury Circular and in any case the Home Office should have sought our previous approval for a Commission, the cost of which is to fall on our Vote'. (S.D. Waley to O.E. Niemeyer, 22 Feb 1921)

The Commission, through its Secretary, applied for a higher rate of expenses for its members when they were away from home, citing as precedent the Commission on Reparations (see no. **178**) whose members received two guineas per head per night rather than the usual twenty-five shillings. This was refused on the grounds that the two Commissions were qualitatively different: the Reparations Commission (like the Defence of the Realm Losses Commission) was considered to be a quasi-judicial body 'expected to function for some time or to perform duties which would naturally carry some remuneration. They are not entirely parallel with an ordinary Commission appointed to do a comparatively short job, membership of which is intended to carry its own reward'. (Treasury memo., 29 June 1921) This was conveyed in the Chancellor's formal reply to the Home Secretary of 2 July 1921. (PRO.T.160/49/E3730)

### 177. Importation of Livestock 1921
App. 11 May 1921. Rep. 30 Aug 1921, Cmd.1139, 1541, xviii. Est. cost £1,601.
Viscount Finlay; Lord Askwith; Sir A.F. Firth; Sir A.E. Shipley; Sir W.H. Peat.
Secretary: A.W. Cockburn. (Barrister)
**To inquire** into the admission into the United Kingdom of livestock for purposes other than immediate slaughter at the ports; and its effects on domestic supplies.

### 178. Reparation Grants 1921-24
App. 15 Aug 1921. Rep. (1) 22 Jan 1923, Cmd.1798, x, 973; (2) 26 Feb 1924, Cmd.2066, ix, 249. Other papers: Non P.P., 1923; 1925; 1926; 1927; 1928; 1929; 1930. Est. cost £2,586.
Lord Sumner; W.E. Horne; J.H. Sabin.
Secretary: J.S. Gardner (Lawyer, Reparation Claims Dept.); resigned Sept 1922; succ. by K.W. Blaxter.
Sabin died 16 March 1922 and was replaced by Sir J.H. Oakley in a Warrant of 20 May 1922.
**To consider** cases where there was a moral claim by British Nationals for compensation for sufferings or damage arising out of the action of the enemy during the War within Annex 1 to Part 8 of the Treaty of Versailles.
PRO.T.160/88/F3243 gives details of way in which the terms of reference were drawn up; it was emphasised that moral claims were to have more weight than the extent of damage; and that the Commission should not be too legal in character.

### 179. London Government 1921-23
App. 24 Oct 1921. Rep. 27 Feb 1923, Cmd.1830, xii, Pt.1, 567. Evidence: Non P.P., Min. of Health, 1923; 1924. Est. cost £3,032.
Viscount Ullswater; Sir R.V. Vassar-Smith; Sir H.C. Monro; Sir A. Gray; E.H. Hiley; G.J. Talbot; N. Chamberlain; R. Donald; E.R. Turton; S. Walsh.
Secretary: M Heseltine. Asst. Sec: J.A. Lawther. (Both of Min. of Health.)

Vassar-Smith resigned Dec 1921, and Chamberlain in Nov 1922; neither was replaced.

**To inquire** and report what, if any, alterations are needed in the local government of the administrative county of London and the surrounding districts, with a view to securing greater efficiency and economy in the administration of local government services and to reducing any inequalities which may exist in the distribution of local burdens as between different parts of the whole area. (In full.)

The majority report was signed by Ullswater, Monro and Turton, and by Gray, subject to a memorandum, and there were two minority reports: the first signed by Hiley and Talbot; and the second by Donald and Walsh.

PRO.HLG.9/2/91002 contains correspondence and papers relating to the appointment of the Commission, including copies of letters to potential members, and from people who wished to be considered as members.

### 180. Honours System 1922

App. 16 Sept 1922. Rep. 22 Dec 1922: 1923 Cmd.1789, xi, 975. Cost £31.10s.
Lord Dunedin; Duke of Devonshire; Lord Denman; A. Henderson; Sir E. Cecil; Sir S.J.G. Hoare; Sir G.C. Marks.
Secretary: J. Rae.

**To advise** on the procedure to be adopted in future to assist the Prime Minister in making recommendations to the monarch of names of persons deserving special honour. (In full.)

Henderson did not sign and wrote a Dissent to the report, to which the other members attached a reply.

### 181. Local Government 1923-29

App. 14 Feb 1923. Rep. (1) 7 Aug 1925: 1924-25, Cmd.2506, xiv, 479; (2) 9 Oct 1928: 1928-29, Cmd.3213, viii, 25; (3) 12 Nov 1929: 1929-30, Cmd.3436, xv, 593. Evidence: Non P.P., Min. of Health, 1923; 1924; 1925; 1928; 1929; 1930. Est. cost £11,982.
Earl of Onslow; Lord Strachie; Sir G.M.W. Macdonogh; Sir W.R.D. Adkins; Sir W. Middlebrook; Sir L. Beard; Sir W.P. Nicholas; W.R.B. Riddell; E.H. Lloyd; A.M. Myers (ktd. 1924); H.G. Pritchard; E.R. Turton; J.L.V.S. Williams.
Secretary: M. Heseltine; succ. by P. Barter, Apr 1928. Asst. Secs: J.A. Lawther and J.D. Castle. (All of Min. of Health.)

Warrants of 5 March 1925 appointed S. Taylor in place of Dent Adkins who died 30 Jan 1925; of 7 June 1926 appointed J. Bond in place of Powell Nicholas who died 10 Apr 1926; of 19 Oct 1926 appointed H.C. Norman in place of Myers who died 9 Oct 1926. Lloyd resigned 14 March 1928 and Turton died 9 May 1929; neither was replaced. The terms of reference were extended to bring Parish councils and Parish meetings within the scope of the inquiry by a Warrant of 4 Aug 1926.

**To enquire** into existing law and procedure relating to the extension of County Boroughs and the creation of new County Boroughs in England and Wales; the effects of this on existing Councils; to investigate relations between Local

Authorities and make general recommendations as to their constitution, areas and functions.

PRO.HLG.8/2/91001 records Treasury concern over the appointment of the Commission. O.E. Niemeyer to the Minister of Health (26 March 1923) pointed out that as Treasury sanction for the Commission had not been obtained before its approval by the King no provision had been made for its expenses in the 1923-24 Estate, and asked that 'the most rigid economy may be enforced in every detail of their work'. The file contains both the subsequent submissions of estimated costs from the Commission as well as Treasury responses, and includes details of their struggle to obtain Treasury approval for the use of a press cutting service at a cost not to exceed three guineas.

PRO.HO.45/156/442222 gives details of the appointment of the Commission and correspondence relating to the legal implications of its recommendations.

### 182. Mining Subsidence 1923-27

App. 15 June 1923. Rep. (1) 21 Dec 1925: 1926, Cmd.2570, xiii, 807; (2) 23 June 1927, Cmd. 2899, xi, 303. Evidence: Non P.P., Mines Dept., 1923; 1924; 1925. Est. cost £3,758.

Viscount Chelmsford; W. Adamson; Sir W.P. Nicholas; G.A. Lewis; G.C.H. Wheler; V. Hartshorn; H.R. Buchanan; R.G. Ellis; H. Jevons; H. Louis; M.F. Maclean; R.F. MacSwinney; F.B. Varley; J.D. Wallis.

Secretary: W.G. Nott-Bower. (Mines Dept.) Asst. Sec: G.C. North. (Min. of Health)

A Warrant of 17 March 1924 appointed Lord Blanesburgh as chairman and E. Morrell and J.C. Welsh as Commissioners in place of Napier, Adamson and Hartshorn who resigned. Powell Nicholas resigned due to ill health shortly before his death in 1926.

To consider the operation of the law relating to the support of the surface of the land by underlying or adjacent minerals ... to enquire into the extent and gravity of the damage caused by subsidence owing to the extraction of minerals, and to report what steps should be taken by legislation or otherwise to remedy any defects or hardships.

### 183. Superior Civil Service in India 1923-24

App. 15 June 1923. Rep. 27 March 1924, Cmd.2128, viii, 607.

Viscount Lee of Fareham; Sir R.H. Craddock; Sir C. Jackson; Sir C.H. Setalvad; Khan Bahadur Sir M. Habibullah; Rai Bahadur H.K. Kaul; D. Petrie; B. Basu; R. Coupland.

Joint Secretaries: S.F. Stewart (Indian Office) and A.W. Street.

Setalvad resigned 22 Oct 1923 and was replaced on 26 Oct 1923 by N.M. Samarth.

To enquire into and make recommendations on (1) the organisation and general conditions of service, financial and otherwise of the superior Civil Services in India; (2) the possibility of transferring any of their present duties and functions to services constituted on a provincial basis; (3) provisions under the Government of India Act for the recruitment of Europeans and Indians.

The report was signed subject to a note by Basu.

**184. National Health Insurance 1924-26**
App. 11 July 1924. Rep. 22 Feb 1926, Cmd.2596, xiv, 311. Evidence: Non P.P., Min. of Health, 1925; 1926. Est. cost £3,831.
Lord Lawrence of Kingsgate; Sir J. Anderson; Sir H.D. Rolleston; Sir A.W. Watson; Sir A. Worley; Sir A.R. Duncan; A.D. Besant; F. Bramley; J. Cook; J. Evans; A. Gray; W. Jones; Mrs F.N.H. Bell; Miss G.M. Tuckwell.
Secretary: E. Hackforth. (Min. of Health) Asst. Sec: J.W. Peck. (Scottish Bd. of Health)
Bramley resigned because of illness 11 March 1925, and was not replaced.
**To inquire** into the scheme of National Health Insurance established by the National Health Insurance Acts, 1911-22, and to report what, if any, alterations, extensions or developments should be made in regard to the scope of that scheme and the administrative, financial and medical arrangements set up under it. (In full.)
The majority report was signed subject to reservations by Duncan and Gray; the minority report was signed by Cook, Evans, Mrs Harrison Bell and Miss Tuckwell.
PRO.PIN.4/203: Misc. Papers includes typescripts of some of the evidence and statements received by the Commission with a list of names, and brief details of the letters received. Some of these are from groups and associations but many are from individual members of the public and cover a wide range of topics from suggestions about the inclusion of slaughtermen under the National Insurance Act (from J. Mortimer, 14 July 1924) to proposals for a dowry for women at marriage (from Mrs H. Blake, 1 Oct 1924).

**185. Lunacy and Mental Disorder 1924-26**
App. 25 July 1924. Rep.7 July 1926, Cmd.2700, xiii, 373. Evidence: Non P.P., Min. of Health, 1926. Est. cost £2,386.
H.P. Macmillan; Earl Russell; Lord E.S.C. Percy; Sir H.D. Rolleston; Sir T. Hutchison (d. 12 Apr 1925); Sir E.V. Hiley; Sir D. Drummond; W.A. Jowitt; F.D. MacKinnon; H. Snell; Mrs A. Mathew; Miss M.J. Symons.
Secretary: P. Barter. (Min. of Health) Asst. Sec: W. Fairley. (Bd. of Control)
A Warrant of 13 Nov 1924 appointed N. Micklem in place of MacKinnon who had resigned on his appointment as a Justice of the High Court. Lord Percy also resigned in Nov 1924 when he was appointed President of the Board of Education, and was not replaced.
(1) **To enquire** as regards England and Wales into the existing law and administrative machinery in connection with the certification, detention and care of persons who are or are alleged to be of unsound mind; (2) To consider as regards England and Wales the extent to which provision is or should be made for the treatment wihtout certification of persons suffering from mental disorder; And to make recommendations. (In full.)
The Commission was established soon after the case of Harnett v. Bond and Adam when Mr Justice Lush found that Harnett had been wrongfully detained

under the current lunatic laws. Following a number of questions by MPs during March and April 1924, including one from Lady Astor asking if the inquiry would include 'a capable woman' (Hansard, 3 March 1924), Treasury approval was granted on 31 May 1924. (PRO.T.160/196) The Commission was given additional powers to summon witnesses and hear evidence on oath under the Tribunals of Inquiry Act, 1921.

### 186. Food Prices 1924-25
App. 29 Nov 1924. Rep. 23 Apr 1925: 1924-25, Cmd.2390, xiii. Evidence: Non P.P., Bd. of Trade, 1924; 1925. Est. cost £1,485.
Sir A.C. Geddes; Sir J.L. MacLeod; Sir R.H. Rew; Sir W.H. Peat; Sir H.J. Mackinder; F.H. Coller; W.T. Layton; G.A. Powell; W.E. Dudley; W. Grant; H.F. Paul; T.H. Ryland; W.R. Smith; I. Stephenson; Dame H.C.I. Gwynne-Vaughan; Mrs E. Snowden.
Secretary: T. St. Quintin Hill. Asst. Secs: E.M.H. Lloyd; H.V. Tennant.
**To enquire** into the conditions prevailing in the wholesale and retail trades in articles of food of general consumption so far as they affect prices, particularly having regard to the difference between the prices received by producers and the prices paid by consumers and to report what action, if any, can usefully be taken. (In full.)
Rew, Stephenson, Layton and Mrs Snowden signed the report subject to reservations. Smith and Ryland each wrote a minority report.

### 187. Indian Currency and Finance 1925-26
App. 25 Aug 1925. Rep. 1 July 1926, Cmd.2687, xii, 501. Evidence: Non P.P., India Office, 1926. Est. cost Rs.3,31,000.
E.H. Young; Sir R. Mookerjee; Sir N.H.Y. Warren; Sir R.A. Mant; Sir M.B. Dadabhoy; Sir H. Strakosch; Sir A.R. Murray; Sir P. Thakurdas; J.C. Coyajee; W.E. Preston.
Joint Secretaries: G.H. Baxter (India Office) and A. Ayangar (Indian Finance Dept).
**To examine** and report on the Indian Exchange and currency system and practice, to consider whether any modifications are desirable in the interests of India, and to make recommendations. (In full.)
Thakurdas signed subject to dissent. Warren attached a note regarding his position as a Managing Governor of the Imperial Bank of India, stressing that he had signed the report in a personal capacity and not as a representative of the Bank.

### 188. Coal Industry 1925-26
App. 5 Sept 1925. Rep. 6 March 1926, Cmd.2600, xiv. Evidence: Non P.P., Mines Dept., 1926. Est. cost £6,171.
Sir H.L. Samuel; Hon. Sir H.A. Lawrence; Sir W.H. Beveridge; K. Lee.
Secretary: C.S. Hurst. Asst. Sec: F.C. Starling. (Both of Mines Dept.) Assessors: W. Brace; A.E. Cutforth; W. Gibson; H.M. Hudspeth; C.H. Lander.
**To inquire** into and report on the economic position of the coal industry and the

conditions affecting it and to make any recommendations for the improvement thereof. (In full.)

**189. Court of Session and Office of Sheriff Principal (Scotland) 1926-27**
App. 26 Jan 1926; RSM, sealed at Edinburgh 30 Jan 1926. Rep. 25 Jan 1927, Cmd.2801, viii. Evidence: Non P.P., Scottish Office, 1927. Est. cost £1,240.
J.A. Clyde; W. Graham (resigned May 1926); Sir J. Adam; J.L. Wark; W. Meff; W.C. Johnston; J.A. Roxburgh; W.J. Taylor; R.C. Thomson; W.M. Whitelaw.
Secretary: E.E. Parker. (Treasury)
**To enquire** into the constitution and jurisdiction of the Court of Session; and into the jurisdiction, powers, duties and functions of the Sheriffs Principal with a view to ascertaining what changes and improvements might be made.
The report was signed subject to reservations from Meff and Thomson.

**190. Agriculture in India 1926-28**
App. 23 Apr 1926. Interim reports: 1-12 in 1927, viii, 595; 13-16, abridged report, and Final Report signed 14 Apr 1928, Cmd.3132, all in 1928, viii. Evidence: Non P.P., India Office, 1927; 1928.    Est. cost Rs.13,72,734 (c.£102,955).
Marquess of Linlithgow; Sir H.S. Lawrence; Sir T. Middleton; Rai Bahadur Sir L.Ganga Ram (d. 10 July 1927); Sir J. MacKenna; H. Calvert; Raja S.K.C.G.N.D. Garu; N.N. Gangulee; L.K. Hyder; B.S. Kamat.
Joint Secretaries: J.A. Madan (Indian Civil Service) and F.W.H. Smith (India Office). Asst. Sec: J.C. McDougall (Indian Agricultural Service). Liaison Officer: Dr D. Clouston (Agricultural Adviser to Govt. of India).
F. Noyce was appointed Assistant Commissioner during the Commission's work in England, in place of Raja Garu who had been unable to acompany them to England.
**To examine** and report on the present conditions of agricultural and rural economy in British India, and to make recommendations for the improvement of agriculture and to promote the welfare and prosperity of the rural population.

**191. Cross-River Traffic in London 1926**
App. 24 July 1926. Rep. 30 Nov 1926, Cmd.2772, xiii, 217. Evidence: Non P.P., Min. of Transport, 1926. Est. cost £2,994.
Viscount Lee of Fareham; Viscount Hambleden; Sir W.H. Dickinson; Sir W. Plender; Sir L. Weaver; C.E. Inglis.
Secretary: E.G. Howarth. (Bd. of Education; named in Warr.) Asst. Sec: J.R. Chambers.
**To survey** the whole problem of cross-river traffic in London; to report what provision should be made to meet future requirements and, in particular, to consider the proposals made in connexion with Waterloo and St. Paul's Bridges. (In full.)

**192. Land Drainage 1927**
App. 22 March 1927. Rep. 5 Dec 1927, Cmd.2993, x, 1049. Evidence: Non P.P.,

Min. of Agriculture & Fisheries, 1927. Est. cost £885.
Lord Bledisloe; Lord Clinton; Sir G.L. Courthope; Sir A.E. Pritchard; Sir G.H. Etherton; Sir J.C. Priestley; F.D.W. Drummond; R.R. Robbins; L. Harvey; J.W. Hills; H.A. Learoyd; W.R. Smith.
Joint Secretaries: H. Meadows and D.B. Toye. Asst. Sec: Hon. A.W.A. Peel.
Lord Clinton resigned 1 July 1927 due to pressure of work following his appointment as Chairman of the Forestry Commission.
**To enquire** into the present law relating to Land Drainage in England and Wales and its administration, and to consider and report whether amendment of the law was needed, and to make recommendations having regard to all the interests concerned.

### 193. Museums and Galleries 1927-30
App. 1 July 1927. Rep. (1) 1 Sept 1928: 1928-29, Cmd.3192, viii, 699; (2) Pt.I, 20 Sept 1929: 1929-30, Cmd.3401, xvi, 431; Pt.II, 1 Jan 1930, Cmd.3463: 1929-30, xvi, 525. Evidence: Non P.P., Art Collections, 1928; 1929. Est. cost £2,862.
Viscount D'Abernon; E.E. Charteris; Sir T.L. Heath; Sir L. Earle; Sir R.T. Glazebrook; Sir G. Macdonald; Sir C. Thomson; Sir W.M. Conway; Sir H.A. Miers; Sir R.C. Witt; A.E. Cowley.
Secretary: J. Beresford (Treasury). Asst. Sec: J.R. Chambers; succ. by J.H. Penson, 14 Nov 1928.
The Commission had wide ranging terms of reference: **to enquire** into and report on the legal position, organisation, administration, accommodation, structural condition of the buildings and general cost of the institutions containing the National Collections in London and Edinburgh and related matters.
The PRO files refer to the need to include provision in the conditions of the Warrant for the Commissioners to make overseas visits. A previous instance is cited (no. **136**) where the relevant clause was omitted and it had been necessary to revoke the original Warrant and reappoint the Commission. (PRO.HO.45/13788/510789)

### 194. London Squares 1927-28
App. 5 Aug 1927. Rep. 11 Sept 1928: 1928-29, Cmd.3196, viii, 111. Evidence: Non P.P., Min. of Health, 1927; 1928. Est. cost £1,051.
Marquess of Londonderry; Sir H.G. Frank; Dame C.B. Bridgeman; Sir G.H. Duckworth; Sir H.F. New; M.L. Gwyer; C.H. Bird; K.P. Vaughan-Morgan; F. Briant; F.W. Hobbs; R.C. Norman; A.G. Prichard; H. Snell; C. Thomas.
Secretary: I.F. Armer. (Min. of Health)
**To inquire** and report on the squares and similar open spaces existing in the area of the Administrative County of London with special reference to the conditions on which they are held and used and the desirability of their preservation as open spaces and to recommend whether any or all of them should be permanently safeguarded against any use detrimental to their character as open spaces and if so, by what means and on what terms and conditions. (In full.)
The report was signed subject to reservations by Frank, Prichard and Snell.

(PRO.HLG.10; HO.45/13060; /512024)

### 195. Indian Education 1927-30
App. 26 Nov 1927. Rep. 12 May 1930: 1929-30, Cmd.3568-9, xi. Other reports: 1929-30, Cmd.3407, x, 535; Cmd.3572, xii. Evidence: Non P.P., 1930. Est. cost £146,000.
Sir J.A. Simon; Viscount Burnham; Lord Strathcona & Mount Royal; Hon. E.C.G. Cadogan; S. Walsh; G.R.L. Fox; C.R. Attlee.
Joint Secretaries: J.W. Bhore (resigned Feb 1930) and S.F. Stewart. Asst. Secs: R.H.A. Carter and E.W. Perry.
A Warrant of 7 Dec 1927 appointed V. Hartshorn in place of Walsh who resigned. Unlike the other Commissions into Indian affairs this had no Indian members.
This was a Statutory Commission established by the provisions of Section 84A of the Government of India Act **to inquire** into and report on the working of the system of Government; the growth of education and the development of representative institutions in British India.

### 196. Transport 1928-30
App. 4 Aug 1928. Rep. (1) 19 July 1929: 1929-30, Cmd.3365, xvii, 835; (2) 18 Oct 1929: 1929-30, Cmd.3416, xvii, 895; (3) 19 Dec 1930: 1930-31, Cmd.3751, xvii, 619. Evidence: Non P.P., Min. of Transport, 1928; 1929; 1930; 1931. Est. cost £7,950.
Sir A.S.T. Griffith-Boscawen; Marquess of Northampton; Earl of Clarendon; Hon. J.J. Astor; Sir M.G. Wallace; Sir E.V. Hiley; Sir W.G. Lobjoit; I. Salmon; H.E. Crawfurd; J. Learmonth; F. Montague; W.R. Smith.
Secretary: R.H. Tolerton. Asst. Sec: A. Spence.
A Warrant of 18 Sept 1929 appointed W. Leach and F.W. Galton in place of Montague and Smith who had resigned.
**To take into consideration** the problems arising out of the growth of road traffic and to report on what measures should be adopted for the control of traffic in Great Britain.
The final report was signed subject to reservations by Lobjoit and Crawfurd; a memorandum by Crawfurd; and additional recommendations by Donald, Galton and Leach.

### 197. Police Powers and Procedure 1928-29
App. 22 Aug 1928. Rep. 16 March 1929: 1928-29, Cmd.3297, ix, 127. Evidence: Non P.P., HO, 1928; 1929. Est. cost £5,350.
Viscount Lee of Fareham; Lord Ebbisham; Sir H.G. Frank; Dame M.L. Talbot; Sir R.W.E.L. Poole; J.T. Brownlie; Miss M. Beavan; F. Pick.
Secretary: E.E. Bridges. (Treasury) Asst. Sec: G.D. Kirwan. (Home Office)
**To consider** the general powers and duties of the police in England and Wales in the investigation of crimes and offences, including the functions of the Director of Public Prosecutions and the police respectively, and to make any necessary recommendations.

One of the primary reasons for establishing the Commission was the widespread concern over police methods of acquiring evidence. This was specifically expressed in the Minority Report of the Tribunal of Investigation (1928, Cmd.3147, xii, 87) into the Police interrogation of Miss Savidge following her arrest, together with Sir L. Money, on a charge of behaviour 'reasonably likely to offend against public decency'. The case was subsequently dismissed with costs against the Police, and questions were raised as to whether the officers concerned were guilty of perjury or a breach of duty.

### 198. Labour in India 1929-31

App. 4 July 1929. Rep. 14 March 1931: 1930-31, Cmd.3883, xi, 571. Evidence: Non P.P., India Office, 1931. Est. costs Rs. 1,050,000 (c.£78,750).
J.H. Whitley; V.S.S. Sastri; Sir E.V. Sassoon; Sir I. Rahimtoola; Sir A.R. Murray; A.G. Clow; K. Ahmed; G.D. Birla; J. Cliff; N.M. Joshi; D.C. Lall; B.M. le P. Power.
Joint Secretaries: S. Lall and A. Dibdin. Asst. Sec: J.H. Green.
There were forty-three male and one female Assistant Commissioners, and nineteen Lady Assessors.
**To enquire** into and report on the existing conditions of labour in industrial undertakings and plantations in British India; on the health, efficiency and standard of living of the workers; and on the relations between employers and employed; and to make recommendations. (In full.)
Rahimtoola did not sign the report as he had been unable to attend the proceedings of the Commission following his election as President of the Legislative Assembly, 17 Jan 1931. The report was signed subject to minutes of reservation by Sassoon and Ahmed. The other members added comments on Sassoon's note.

### 199. Licensing (England and Wales) 1929-31

App. 30 Sept 1929. Rep. 17 Dec 1931: 1931-32, Cmd.3988, xi, 573. Evidence: Non P.P., HO, 1929; 1930; 1931; 1932. Est. Cost £19,050.
Lord Amulree; Sir J. Pedder; Sir E.F. Stockton; T.G. Arnold; Mrs E. Barton; W.D. Bentliff; G.A. Bryson; H. Carter; A.A.H. Findlay; J. Fitton; G.A. France; B.T. Hall (d. 10 Jan 1931); W.L. Hichens; A. Jenkins; J.J. Mallon; J. Morgan; Miss E. Neville; A. Sherwell; Mrs S.D. Simon; T. Skurray; F.P. Whitbread.
Secretary: M.H. Whitelegge. Asst. Sec: T. Hutson. (Both of Home Office.)
A Warrant of 3 Jan 1930 appointed R.T. Jones in place of Findlay who had resigned in Dec 1929.
**To inquire** into the working of the laws relating to the sale and supply of intoxicating liquors, and into the social and economic aspects of the question, and to examine and report upon proposals that may be made for amending the law in England and Wales in the public interest. (In full.)
The majority report was signed subject to reservations by Stockton, Carter, Fitton, Hichens, Miss Neville and Skurray. There were three separate minority reports by Mrs Simon; Morgan; and Whitbread.

**200. Civil Service 1929-31**
App. 28 Oct 1929. Rep. 8 July 1931: 1930-31, Cmd.3909, x, 517. Evidence: Non P.P., Treasury, 1929; 1930; 1931; 1932. Est. cost £14,155.
Lord Tomlin; Duchess of Atholl; Sir C.T. Needham; Sir H. Sharp; Sir P.R. Jackson; Sir A. Pownall; J.B. Baillie; W. Cash; F.W. Goldstone; Mrs B.A. Gould; Miss M.A. Hamilton; Mrs E.M. Lowe; T.E. Naylor; P.J. Pybus; R. Richards; Mrs M. Wintringham.
Secretary: E.E. Bridges. Asst. Sec: H. Parker. (Both of the Treasury.)
A Warrant of 8 Nov 1929 appointed J. Bromley in place of Naylor who had resigned.
**To enquire** into and report on (a) the structure and organisation of and (b) the conditions of service in and retirement from the Civil Service. The terms of reference made specific reference to the position of women civil servants.

**201. Licensing Laws in Scotland 1929-31**
App. 28 Oct 1929. Rep. 25 May 1931: 1930-31, Cmd.3894, xv, 423. Evidence: Non P.P., 1930; 1931. Est. cost £4,000. (LP)
Hon. Lord Mackay; Hon. J. Dewar (Lord Forteviot, 1929); Hon. Mrs L. Forrester-Paton; Sir A.J.W. Lewis; Sir R. Stewart; J.H. Miller; J. Fraser; P. Chalmers; A.B. Clarke; O. Coyle; Mrs A. Hardie; W. McKim; R.O. Pagan; W.E. Whyte (ktd. 1930).
Secretary: T.B. Simpson. (Advocate) Asst. Sec: W.H. Blacklock. (Scottish Office)
**To investigate** the whole field of legislation relating to the sale and supply of exciseable liquor in Scotland, and to report what amendment in the law, if any, is desirable in the public interest. (In full.)
The majority report was signed subject to reservations by Miller and McKim; and the minority Report was signed by the Hon. Mrs Forrester-Paton, Mrs Hardie, Stewart and Chalmers.

**202. Unemployment Insurance 1930-32**
App. 9 Dec 1930. Rep. (1) 1 June 1931: 1930-31, Cmd.3872, xvii, 885; (2) 27 Oct 1932: 1931-32, Cmd.4185, xiii, 393. Evidence: Non P.P., Min. of Labour, 1931; 1932; 1933. Est. cost £14,091.
H.H. Gregory; W. Asbury; H. Clay; H.J.W. Hetherington; E.C.P. Lascelles; Mrs C.D. Rackham; H.M. Trouncer.
Secretary: H.C. Emmerson. Asst. Sec: H.R. Hodges.
**To enquire** into the provisions and working of the Unemployment Insurance Scheme and to make recommendations with regard to (1) its future scope, the provisions which it should contain and the means by which it may be made solvent and self-supporting, and, (2) the arrangements which should be made outside the scheme for the unemployed who are capable of and available for work. (In full.)
The first report was signed by Gregory, Clay, Hetherington, Lascelles and Trouncer, subject to a note by Clay and Trouncer. A minority report was issued by Asbury and Mrs Rackham, with a note by Asbury expressing agreement with the majority on the position of married women under the Unemployment

Insurance Acts, but with a further note by Mrs Rackham recording her disagreement with her colleagues in this matter. The final report was also split: Clay and Trouncer signed the majority report subject to a note and a reservation respectively; and Asbury and Mrs Rackham produced a minority report.

### 203. Malta 1931-32
App. 7 Apr 1931. Rep. 29 Jan 1932: 1931-32, Cmd.3993, vi, 819. Costs from Malta Funds.

Lord Askwith; Sir W. Egerton; Count de Salis.

Secretary: A.J. Dawe. (Colonial Office)

**To make full and diligent enquiry** into the existing political situation in the Island of Malta and to put forward recommendations as to the steps which can and should be taken for its amelioration. (In full.)

### 204. Lotteries 1932-33
App. 4 June 1932. Rep. (1) 5 Jan 1933, Cmd.4234, xiv, 349; (2) 1 June 1933: 1932-33, Cmd.4341, xiv, 349. Evidence: Non P.P., 1932; 1933. Est. cost £3,400.

Sir S.A.T. Rowlatt; Lady Emmott; Sir F.S. Jackson; C.T. Cramp; R.F. Graham-Campbell; W.L. Hichens; Sir J. Leishman; A. Maitland; Sir D.J. Owen; A. Shaw; Sir S.M. Skinner; Mrs M.D. Stocks.

Secretary: E.E. Bridges (Treasury). Asst. Sec: A. Johnston. (HO)

**To enquire** into the existing law and the practice thereunder relating to lotteries, betting, gambling and cognate matters, and to report what changes, if any, are desirable and practicable. (In full.)

### 205. Newfoundland 1933
App. 17 Feb 1933. Rep. 4 Oct 1933: 1933-34, Cmd.4480, xiv, 357. Related papers: Cmd.4479, same vol., 661. Est. cost of U.K. share £2,345.

Lord Amulree; C.A. Magrath; Sir W.E. Stavert.

Secretary: P.A. Clutterbuck. (Dominions Office; named in Warr.)

**To examine** into the future of Newfoundland and in particular to report on the financial situation and prospects therein.

### 206. University of Durham 1934-35
App. 16 March 1934. Rep. 22 Jan 1935: 1934-35, Cmd.4815, viii, 489. Est. cost £1,868.

Lord Moyne; Countess Grey; Sir W.R. Barker; A.G. Church; H.R. Dean; F.H. Dudden; T.F. Sibly; W. Spens.

Secretary: S.H. Wood.

**To enquire** into the organisation and work of the University of Durham and its constituent colleges and into the relation of the University to those colleges, and to report on any desirable changes or improvements.

### 207. Tithe Rentcharge in England and Wales 1934-36
App. 27 Aug 1934. Rep. 26 Nov 1935: 1935-36, Cmd.5095, xiv, 859. Evidence: Non P.P., 1935; 1936. Est. cost £1,652.

Sir J.F. Williams; Lord Cornwallis (d. 26 Sept 1935); Sir E.R. Peacock; Sir L.J. Coates; Sir J.E. Lloyd.
Secretary: E.L. Mitchell. Asst. Sec: A.S. Allen.
**To enquire** into and report upon the whole question of tithe rentcharge in England and Wales and its incidence.
The majority report was signed by Williams and Lloyd and subject to a reservation by Peacock. Coates issued a minority report. Cmd.5102 was printed with the report and sets out government proposals to revise and amend the tithe rentcharge scheme.

### 208. Common Law 1934-36
App. 5 Dec 1934. Rep. 20 Jan 1936: 1935-36, Cmd.5065, viii, 105. Evidence: Non P.P., 1935. Est. cost £564.
Earl Peel; Lord Hanworth; Sir C. Schuster; J.G. Archibald; E.C. Davies; W.T. Monckton; H.L. Murphy.
Joint Secretaries: J. Foster and G.P. Humphreys-Davies. Asst. Sec: Miss A. M. Fletcher. (The first woman to be appointed in this position.)
**To enquire** into the state of business in the King's Bench Division of the High Court of Justice and to report whether, with a view to greater despatch, any reforms should be adopted.
The report was signed subject to notes by Hanworth and Schuster; and a memorandum by Davies.

### 209. Arms Trade 1935-36
App. 19 Feb 1935. Rep. 24 Sept 1936: 1935-36, Cmd.5292, vii, 483. Evidence: Non P.P., 1935; 1936. Est. cost £7,341.
Sir J.E. Bankes; Sir P.H. Gibbs; Dame R.E. Crowdy; Sir T.W. Allen; Sir K. Lee; H.C. Gutteridge; J.A. Spender.
Secretary: E. Twentyman. Asst. Sec: D. Haigh.
The commission was reissued following the accession of Edward VIII, 10 Feb 1936 under a composite Warrant 'ratifying and confirming the terms of various commissions of enquiry issued in the reign of his late Majesty'.
**To consider** and report upon the practicability and desirability of a prohibition of the private manufacture of, and trade in, arms; and the institution of a state monopoly; and to examine present United Kingdom arrangements.

### 210. Local Government in Tyneside 1935-37
App. 1 May 1935. Rep. 23 Feb 1937: 1936-37, Cmd.5402, xiii,117. Est. cost £1,470.
Sir S.A.T. Rowlatt; Sir A.N. Scott; C.H. Roberts.
Secretary: A.S. Charlton.
Rowland resigned and a Warrant of 12 Dec 1935 appointed Scott as Chairman, and W.B. Couchman; Lord Merthyr; G. Clark and H. Barrow to the Commission. Further warrants of 10 Feb 1936 and 17 Dec 1936 reappointed the Commission following the accession and subsequent abdication of Edward VIII. This led to considerable delays in the Commission's work and they did not hold their first

meeting until 18 Feb 1936. PRO.HLG.11/3 records the detailed correspondence between the Secretary and the members of the Commission on this and other matters.

**To examine** the system of local government in the areas north and south of the River Tyne, and to consider and recommend any changes necessary to secure greater economy and efficiency.

Roberts issued a minority report.

### 211. Merthyr Tydfil 1935

App. 1 May 1935. Rep. 12 Nov 1935: 1935-36, Cmd.5039, xiv. Est. cost £497.

Sir A.B. Lowry; J.T. Richards.

Secretary: P.F.G. Robinson. (Min. of Health)

**To investigate** and report whether Merthyr Tydfil should continue to hold the status of a county borough, and if not, to recommend alternative arrangements.

### 212. Safety in Coal Mines 1935-38

App. 14 Dec 1935. Rep. 2 Dec 1938: 1938-39, Cmd.5890, xiii, 263. Evidence: Non P.P., 1936; 1937; 1938. Est. cost £14,940.

Lord Rockley; Sir M. Delevingne; Sir H. Walker; D.R. Grenfell; G.C. Allsebrook; E.O.F. Brown; E. Edwards; W.T. Miller; W.H. Telfer; J. Walker.

Secretary: E.W. Ravenshear. Asst. Sec: G.B. Brown.

Warrants of 10 Feb 1936 and 17 Dec 1936 reappointed the Commission following the accession and subsequent abdication of Edward VIII.

**To inquire** whether the safety and health of mine workers could be better ensured by extending or modifying the principles or general provisions of the Coal Mines Act, 1911, and to make recommendations.

The report was signed subject to reservations by Brown, Edwards, Telfer and Walker.

### 213. Palestine 1936-37

App. 7 Aug 1936. Rep. 22 June 1937: 1936-37, Cmd.5479, xiv, 231. Evidence: Non P.P., Colonial Office, 1937. Est. cost £4,050.

Earl Peel; Sir H.G.M. Rumbold; Sir E.L.L. Hammond; Sir W.M. Carter; Sir H. Morris; R. Coupland.

Secretary: J.M. Martin. (Colonial Office)

The Commission was reappointed by Warrant of 17 Dec 1936 following the accession of George VI.

**To ascertain** the underlying causes of the disturbances which broke out in Palestine in the middle of April 1936; to enquire into the manner in which the Mandate for Palestine was being implemented, and to make recommendations.

The Arab Higher Committee boycotted the proceedings of the Commission which had no power to compel their co-operation. Cmd.5513, published with the report, is a Statement of Policy by the UK Government.

### 214. Distribution of the Industrial Population 1937-39

App. 8 July 1937. Rep. pres. 16 Jan 1940: 1939-40, Cmd.6153, iv, 263*.

Evidence: Non P.P., 1937; 1938; 1939. Est. cost £10,627.
Sir M. Barlow; Sir W.A. Robinson; Sir F. L'Estrange Joseph; Sir W.E. Whyte; L.P. Abercrombie; E. Bevin; F. D'Arcy Cooper; Mrs H. Hichens; Mrs M.N. Hill; J.H. Jones; G.P. Morris; S.A. Smith; G.W. Thomson.
Secretary: J. Leader. Asst. Sec: N.C. Rowland.
A warrant of 23 June 1938 appointed H.H. Elvin in place of Bevin who had resigned.
**To inquire** into the causes which had influenced the present geographical distribution of the industrial population of Great Britain and the probable direction of any future changes; its social, economic, or strategic disadvantages, and to report on any remedial measures that should be taken in the national interest.
The majority report was signed subject to reservations by Whyte, Jones and Thomson. The minority report was signed by Abercrombie, Elvin and Mrs Hichens, with a further dissentient note related to the majority report by Abercrombie.
Statistical data was supplied by Manchester University.
*The report was completed in August 1939 but was not printed and signed until December 1939.

### 215. Rhodesia and Nyasaland 1938-39
App. 9 March 1938. Rep. 1 March 1939: 1938-39, Cmd.5949, xv, 211. Est. cost £5,015.
Viscount Bledisloe; P.A. Cooper; E. Evans; T. Fitzgerald; W.H. Mainwaring; I.L. Orr-Ewing.
Secretary: G.F. Seel. (Named in Warr.) Asst. Sec: N. Pritchard.
**To enquire** and report whether any, and if so, what, form of closer co-operation or association between Southern Rhodesia, Northern Rhodesia and Nyasaland was desirable and feasible, with due regard to the interest of all the inhabitants, irrespective of race.
The report was signed by all the members, but each of them added notes.

### 216. West Indies 1938-39
App. 5 Aug 1938. Rep. 16 Feb 1940: 1939-40, Cmd.6174, v, 561; 21 Dec 1939: 1944-45, Cmd.6607, vi, 245. Cmd.6608, same vol., is a separate report by Professor Engledow on Agriculture, Fisheries, Forestry and Veterinary Matters. Est. UK cost £13,454.
Lord Moyne; Sir R.E. Stubbs; Dame R.E. Crowdy; Sir W.M. Citrine; Sir P.G. Mackinnon; R. Assheton; Dr M.G. Blacklock; F.L. Engledow; H.D. Henderson; M. Jones (d. 23 Apr 1939).
Secretary: T.I.K. Lloyd. Asst. Sec: C.Y. Carstairs. (Both named in Warr.)
Assheton resigned when he was appointed Parliamentary Secretary to the Ministry of Labour and National Service, 6 Sept 1939.
**To investigate** social and economic conditions in Barbados, British Guiana, British Honduras, Jamaica, the Leeward Islands, Trinidad and Tobago, and the Windward Islands, and matters connected therewith, and to make recommendations. (In full.)
The full report was not published until 1945: Cmd.6174 contains only the

recommendations of the Commission. M. MacDonald, Secretary of State for the Colonies, informed Lord Moyne (13 Feb 1940) that the report submitted to His Majesty on 21 Dec 1939 was not be published at the present time but the government wished to carry out its major recommendations. To this end MacDonald asked the Commission to prepare a statement of these to serve as a guide for those involved in West Indian affairs until the full report could be published. The statement was sent to the Secretary of State on 16 Feb 1940.

Some parts of the Commission's enquiries were more than usually public: the report includes photographs of crowds in Queen's Park, Bridgetown, Barbados where the proceedings of Commission were broadcast.

### 217. Workmen's Compensation 1938-44

App. 22 Dec 1938. Rep. 22 Dec 1944: 1944-45, Cmd.6588, vi, 779. Evidence: Non P.P., 1939; 1940. Est. cost £8,459.

Sir H.J.W. Hetherington; W. Stewart; R.R. Bannatyne; E. Hackforth; C.T.A. Sadd; R.C. Elmslie (d. 24 July 1940); J.S. Boyd; A.B. Cauty; Miss G. Drysdale; G.A. Isaacs; W. Lawther; J.A. Lillie; J.L. Smyth; F.J. Williams; W.D. Woolley; Mrs B.F. Wootton.

Secretary: F. Popplewell.

**To inquire** into and report on the operation and effects of the system of workmen's compensation for injuries due to employment and the working and scope of the law relating thereto.

The Commission suspended its work in early 1940 and the reports were amalgamated with those of various other committees between 1938 and 1945, in particular the Inter-Departmental Committee into Social Insurance appointed in June 1941 (Chairman Sir William Beveridge). Cmd.6588 refers to these and contains only a brief summary report of the Commission's activities. The Commission was requested by the Secretary of State to remain in being until a satisfactory scheme for compensation had been worked out. Following the publication of the White Papers on Social Insurance and the report of the Committee on Social Insurance (Chairman Sir Walter Monckton) the Royal Commission was terminated.

# Appendix 1

## I. Exhibitions

### 1. Vienna 1872-74
App. 29 Apr 1872. Chairman: Prince of Wales; Secretary: F.P.C. Owen. Rep. 12 June 1874, C.1072-1-iv, lxxiii, Parts I-IV.

### 2. Paris 1877-80
App. 22 Jan 1877. President: Prince of Wales; Secretary: F.P.C. Owen. Rep. 1880, C.2588, xxxii.

### 3. Sydney & Melbourne 1879-81
App. 5 Apr 1879. President: Prince of Wales; Secretary: T.A. Wright. Rep. 19 Dec 188, C.3099, xxviii.

### 4. Indian & Colonial 1884-87
App. 8 Nov 1884. President: Prince of Wales; Secretary: F.P.C. Owen. Rep. 30 Apr 1887, C.5083, xx.

### 5. Adelaide (South Australia) 1886-88
App. 29 Oct 1886. Chairman: Duke of Cambridge; Secretary: Sir H.B. Sandford. Rep. 1888, C.5440, xxiv.

### 6. Melbourne (Victoria) 1887-88
App. 3 Oct 1887. Hon. President: Prince of Wales; Chairman: Earl of Rosebery. Secretary: Major H. Jekyll. Rep. 1889, C.5848, xxxiv, 473.

### 7. Chicago 1891
App. 26 Aug 1891. The *London Gazette* of 28 Aug 1891 records that a Warrant was issued to the President, Vice Presidents, Treasurers and other Members of the Council of the Society for the encouragement of Arts, Manufactures and Commerce. The Secretary was Sir H.T. Wood. No report was recorded.

### 8. Hobart (Tasmania) 1894
App. 3 May 1894. President: Marquess of Ripon; Secretary: G.C. Levey. No report was recorded.

### 9. Paris 1898-1901
App. 1 Feb 1898. President: Prince of Wales; Secretary: Major H. Jekyll. Rep. 1901, Cd.629-30, xxxi. Following the accession of the Prince of Wales to the throne as Edward VII, the Duke of Devonshire was appointed President and Chairman by Warrant of 14 March 1901.

### 10. St Louis 1903-06
App. 23 Apr 1903. President : Prince of Wales; Chairman: Viscount Peel; Secretary: C.M. Watson. Rep. 1906, Cd.2800, liv, 297.

**11. Brussels, Rome & Turin 1909-11**
App. 19 March 1909. President: Prince of Wales; Chairman: Earl of Lytton; Secretary: U.F. Wintour. Rep. 1913: 1912-13, Cd.6609, xxii.

**II. Permanent or Semi-Permanent Commissions**

**12. Historical Documents 1869**
App. 2 Apr 1869. Lord Romilly. 1st rep. 1870, C.55, xxxix, 543. Still sitting; now known as Commission on Historical Manuscripts.

**13. Horse Breeding 1887-1911**
App. 3 Dec 1887. Duke of Portland. 1st rep. 1888, C.5419, xlviii; Final rep. 1911, Cd.5936, xxix.

**14. Crofter Colonisation 1888-1906**
App. 24 Dec 1888. Marquess of Lothian. 1st rep. 1890, C.6067, xxvii, 237; Final rep. 1906, Cd.3145, xcvii.

**15. Ancient Monuments in Scotland 1908**
App. 7 Feb 1908. Sir H.E. Maxwell. 1st rep. 1909, Cd.4770, x, 137.

**16. Ancient Monuments in Wales & Monmouthshire 1908**
App. 10 Aug 1908. Sir John Rhys. 1st rep. 1910, Cd.5285, ix, 207.

**17. Ancient Monuments in England 1908**
App. 27 Oct 1908. Lord Burghclere. 1st rep. 1910, Cd.5367, xxxvi, 727. This Commission was reappointed by Warrant of 26 May 1910 on the accession of George V.

**18. Awards to Inventors 1919-37**
App. 19 March 1919. Sir C.H. Sargant. 1st rep., 1921, Cmd. 1112, viii, 507. Final rep., 1937-38, Cmd.5594, xii, 639.

**19. Fine Art 1924**
App. 30 May 1924. Earl of Crawford & Balcarres. 1st rep., 1924, Cmd.2228, ix, 609.

**III. Dardanelles & Mesopotamia 1916-19**
This was a Special Commission, but is often listed as a Royal Commission. Its was appointed under the Special Commissions (Dardanelles & Mesopotamia) Act, 1916 (6 & 7 Geo V) 17 Aug 1916, which invoked the combined authority of Monarch and Parliament **to inquire** into the origin, inception and conduct of operations of war in the Dardanelles and Mesopotamia.

## 20. Dardanelles 1916-19

Rep. (1) 12 Feb 1917: 1917-18, Cd.8490, Cd.8502, x, 419; (2) 4 Dec 1917: 1919, Cmd., 371, xiii, 715.

Earl of Cromer (d. 29 Jan 1917); A. Fisher; Sir T. Mackenzie; Sir F. Cawley; J.A. Clyde; S.L. Gwynn; W. Roch; Sir W.H. May*; Lord Nicholson*; W. Pickford*.

Secretary: E.G. Mears.

Pickford was appointed chairman after the death of the Earl of Cromer. Clyde and Cawley resigned when they took up the positions of Lord Advocate and Chancellor of the Duchy of Lancaster respectively.

The first report was signed with dissenting notes by Fisher and Mackenzie. Roch did not sign and attached a memorandum. The report was censored at its first publication, and some of the material was reinserted in the supplemental report, Cd.8502.

## 21. Mesopotamia 1916-17

Rep. 17 May 1917: 1917-18, Cd.8610, xvi, 773.

Lord G.F. Hamilton; Earl of Donoughmore; Lord H. Cecil; Sir A. Williamson; J. Hodge; J.C. Wedgwood; Sir C.A.G. Bridge*; Sir N.G. Lyttelton*.

Secretary: R.G. Duff. Asst. Sec. J.W. Fitzwilliam.

Wedgwood did not sign, and wrote a dissenting report.

*These appointments were made under the terms of the Act which required that at least one naval and one military officer from the retired lists should serve on each Commission.

## IV. Election Commissions (Enquiries into electoral corruption)

| | | |
|---|---|---|
| 1870 | Beverley | C.15-16, xxix |
| | Bridgwater | C.10-12, xxx |
| | Cashel, Ireland | C.9, xxxii |
| | Dublin | C.93-i, xxxiii |
| | Norwich | C.13-14, xxxi |
| | Sligo | C.48, xxxii, 621 |
| 1876 | Boston | C.1441-i, xxviii |
| | Norwich | C.1442-i, xxvii |
| 1881 | Boston | C.2784, xxxviii |

| | | |
|---|---|---|
| | Canterbury | C.2775, xxxix |
| | Chester | C.2824, xl |
| | Gloucester | C.2841, xli |
| | Knaresborough | C.2777, xlii |
| | Macclesfield | C.2853, xliii |
| | Oxford | C.2856, xliv |
| | Sandwich | C.2796, xlv |
| 1906 | Worcester | Cd.3268-9, xcv, 95 |

# Appendix 2

Committee meetings can be long, and sometimes less than fascinating, which is perhaps why one member of the Irish sub-committee of the Royal Commission on Sugar was inspired to write the following Valedictory verses which he presented to the secretary, a Mr Gladwell. (7 Dec 1918, included in his letter to J. St Loe Strachey: Strachey Papers, S/30/10, Reprinted by kind permission of the House of Lords Record Office.)


"Cras ingens"

Ah what avails the sceptred race?
Ah what the form divine?
Late precedents I now embrace,
Like Wilhelm, I resign.
I lay aside my wreath of bays,
My dream of state I doff,
As Robey succulently says
"In other words - pop off".


No longer shall I make the laws
Or break them in bravado
Or tell a trader he's no cause
For scorning Muscovado.
Who e'er dislikes his sugar brown
Must either "lump" or "lave" it.
I flee from the retailers' frown
To file an affidavit.


The friends I had are in a huff
Because, with zest unswerving,
I gave not one of them enough
Of sugar for preserving.
And now, when I meet Jack or Sam,
And genial warmth elates me,
I see him wondering who I am,
And why on earth he hates me.

# APPENDIX

Had I but served my God with half
The zeal I served Committees,
My Guinness I might freely quaff
Gratis, in several cities.
Now you alone, who still wade through
The complicated mess that
I've just escaped, may sigh "Adieu!
In pace - requiescat".

F.C. Stewart Moore

# Index of Officials

All references are to serial numbers in the text and not to page numbers

# Index of Commissions

All references are to serial numbers in the text and not to page numbers

Accidents in Mines (1879-81), 32
Accidents to Railway Servants (1899-1900), 102
Administration in the Army and Navy (1888-90), 69
Aged Poor (1893-95), 82
Agricultural Depression (1893-97), 86
Agricultural Industry in Great Britain (1919), 173
Agricultural Interests (1879-82), 35
Agriculture in India (1926-28), 190
Alien Immigration (1902-03), 110
Allegations against Sir John Jackson, Limited (1916-17), 168
Arms Trade (1935-36), 209
Army Officers (1873-74), 9
Army Promotion (1874-76), 12
Arrest and Subsequent Treatment of Mr F.S. Skeffington, Mr T. Dickson and Mr P.J. McIntyre (1916), 166
Arsenical Poisoning (1901-03), 106

Blind, Deaf and Dumb (1885-89), 56

Canals and Inland Navigation (1906-11), 126
Care and Control of the Feeble-Minded (1904-08), 120
Cathedral Churches (1879-85), 34
Church in Scotland Act (1905-09), 123
Church in Wales (1906-10), 131
Churches in Scotland (1904-05), 121
City of London Charities (1878-80), 29
City of London Livery Companies (1880-84), 39
Civil Establishments (1886-87), 59
Civil Service (1912-15), 150
Civil Service (1929-31), 200
Coal Industry (1919), 172
Coal Industry (1925-26), 188
Coal Supply (1901-05), 109
Coast Erosion (1906-11), 132
Colonial Defences (1879-82), 36
Common Law (1934-36), 208
Congestion in Ireland (1906-08), 133
Control of trade from tuberculous animals (1896-98), 93
Copyright (1875-78), 17
Court of Session and Office of Sheriff Principal (Scotland) (1926-27), 189
Crofters and Cottars in Highlands and Islands of Scotland (1883-84), 52
Cross-River Traffic in London (1926), 191

Decimal Coinage (1918-20), 170
Defence of the Realm (1915-20), 162

# INDEX OF COMMISSIONS

# INDEX OF COMMISSIONS

# INDEX OF COMMISSIONS